ADVICE TO BE
#UNBREAKABLE

TONY JACOBSEN

Advice to Be #UNBREAKABLE

Your Guide to Overcoming Challenges, Embracing Uniqueness, and Cultivating a Mindset of Resilience and Positivity!

Written by Tony Jacobsen

First Edition, 2024 Published by Egg Sandwich Media | #UNBREAKABLE

Cover Design by Tony Jacobsen, Teemaree, and Rob Williams.

www.tonyjacobsen.com
www.advicetobeunbreakable.com

Published in the United States of America

Paperback: ISBN 979-8-9907564-1-0
Ebook: ISBN 979-8-9907564-0-3
Hardcover: ISBN 979-8-9907564-2-7

Acknowledgements

I can't do what I do without you, Teemaree.
I love you. Thank you for being my person.

To all of my clients—past, present, and future—you help
me understand what it means to be #UNBREAKABLE.

Also by Tony Jacobsen

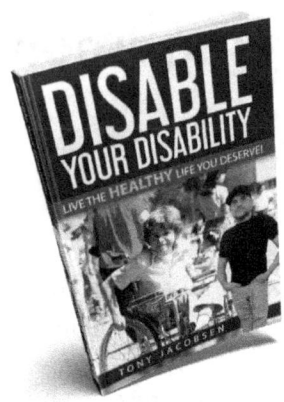

"Disable Your Disability: Live the Healthy Life You Deserve!"

An encouraging book for people with physical limitations and disabilities who want to learn how to get and stay healthier!

Available in hardcover, paperback, ebook, and audio at www.tonyjacobsen.com

"Many receive advice, only the wise profit from it."
-Harper Lee

"Where there is strife, there is pride, but wisdom is found in those who take advice."
Proverbs 13:10 NIV

"You will break. But, luckily, that's when the healing starts!"
-Tony Jacobsen

Contents

Time to Unlock Your #UNBREAKABLE Life

Let's begin with an exercise. No, I won't make you do push-ups or bicep curls. That's for later.

This exercise is for your mind. Here we go.

Can you think of a time in your life when you were broken?

I'm sure answering this question was relatively easy. Perhaps an exact moment flooded back from your past, or maybe you instantly thought about your current situation.

Whatever the case may be, you're not alone. We all break. And with those breaks, we all face the frustrations, disappointments, and pains associated with them.

But I'm here to show you how not to get discouraged by your broken moments and give you the tools necessary to fully embrace everything you are—from your past to your present—so you can define your future self!

We all have the opportunity to live an #UNBREAKABLE life, so let's take advantage of this fantastic opportunity!

Welcome to the unique world of "Advice to Be #UNBREAKABLE," a book that combines all the aspects of my life as an author, speaker, fitness coach, and DJ and reveals the power of not only embracing my disability but much more, to live a powerful life. This is not just a book; it's an invitation to discover your limitless potential, rise above challenges, and live a life that knows no bounds.

In these pages, I share with you the hard-won wisdom gained and life lessons learned from my years of experience in multiple domains of life. I've dedicated years to refining these #UNBREAKABLE concepts, drawing from my diverse background in entertainment, personal development, coaching, and the dynamic world of music and DJing. My experiences have shaped my unique and sometimes controversial perspective, and I'm excited to share my knowledge and expertise with you.

The principles presented here can help you redefine your life and empower you to step into greatness. Each chapter holds a key to personal growth, resilience, and a renewed sense of purpose.

Now, let me tell you what this book isn't about. It isn't about avoiding challenges or pretending that life is always smooth sailing. Instead, it's about understanding that breaking is a natural part of life and that what matters most is how we redefine ourselves after facing adversity.

Life teaches us invaluable lessons through our hardships—the pains we never wish to revisit. This book is about learning from those experiences, arming ourselves with newfound wisdom, and forging a significantly less demanding and painful path.

You might wonder why I chose the hashtag and all capital letters in #UNBREAKABLE. Let me explain. The hashtag symbol (#)—or what my generation would call a "pound sign"—is a familiar sight on social media, used to discover, categorize and organize content. By hashtagging the word, I aim to make the statement, the movement, this book, and everything associated with it easily recognizable, catchy, memorable, and simple to locate.

But there's more to it than just digital relevance. "UNBREAKABLE" is written in all caps to emphasize its significance. It represents the core of everything I am, and I know you can be too! It's about discovering inner strength to conquer obstacles, no matter how daunting they may seem.

Whether you seek motivation, encouragement, inspiration, a shift in perspective, or the wisdom to conquer your dreams, "Advice to Be #UNBREAKABLE" is your personal growth toolkit.

Throughout these pages, I'm sharing 40 bite-sized, easily digestible, life-changing lessons, insights from personal stories, and practical advice you can immediately implement. I'll also show you the power of mindset, the significance of asking for help, the art of perseverance and resilience, the magic in embracing uniqueness, and the extraordinary power of collaboration.

And much…much…more.

As you start this adventure, I want you to know that this book is not just a one-time read—it's a journey of continuous growth. You'll discover the power of flipping the script, turning self-criticism into self-belief, and rewriting your narrative. Embrace the experience, revisit these pages, and apply these insights as you grow into the best version of yourself.

Your journey begins now. Life is filled with challenges, but you're not alone. As your guide, mentor, and fellow traveler, I'm here to inspire, empower, and support you every step of the way.

It's time to be #UNBREAKABLE.

Why Me?

"Why should I listen to you?" you might wonder. It's a valid question, and I'm honored to share my story with you. My life has been filled with challenges and accomplishments. Through the highs and lows, I've changed my life and empowered countless others to live healthier, more fulfilling lives despite their limitations.

Starting With a Rare Bone Disorder

My life began with a unique challenge that solidified the meaning of being "broken" and the subsequent feelings associated with it.

I was born with Osteogenesis Imperfecta (O.I.), a rare brittle bone disease that means my bones are more susceptible to fractures. That's the simple explanation, but there's more to it. It's a collagen disorder that can affect every part of my body. I've suffered through 75+ bone fractures. Along with the fractures, I've undergone 12 surgical procedures, most of which were to implant or replace metal rods from the four long bones in my legs. I still have them to this day! So, yes, I know what it's like to be broken in many different ways.

My life has had me face some pretty severe physical and emotional challenges that truly put me to the test. I used a wheelchair throughout my childhood. I walked on crutches through my late teens and early 20s. And it wasn't until I was 24 years old, fresh off one of my last rod-replacement surgeries, that I would take my very first unassisted steps. Learning to walk as a young adult wasn't easy, especially since I had been denying the circumstances that had put me there.

My denial lasted another 20 years. And with it came heftier challenges and many broken moments: physically, emotionally, mentally.

Then, it all finally came to a head. One of the biggest challenges occurred when I was 42 years old. I underwent a profound physical transformation that forced me to confront my disability head-on. I wrote about it in my first book, "Disable Your Disability: Live the Healthy Life You Deserve!". It was during this period that I learned the power of embracing my disability and shifting my focus to proper exercise, nutrition, and a complete mindset overhaul to live a healthier and happier life.

Looking back, I could have easily let this condition define me, and it did for many years. But luckily, after learning how to work on myself genuinely, I made a conscious choice. I decided that I wouldn't let my disability be a limitation; instead, I would use it as a source of strength.

As I said, my transformation sparked a revelation in me and my entire life. It led to the creation of my book, "Disable Your Disability: Live the Healthy Life You Deserve!" In its pages, I tell my story from birth to breakthrough, and I share the invaluable lessons I learned along the way to embracing my disability and living a healthier life. Little did I know that my book would become a beacon of hope for countless individuals seeking to break free from the limitations imposed by disabilities.

The impact of "Disable Your Disability" resonated beyond the written word. Inspired to help others embrace their unique strengths and alter their lives, I pursued my passion further. I became a NASM certified personal trainer dedicated to guiding individuals with disabilities and other limitations toward physical empowerment.

I've successfully coached hundreds in-person and virtually through one-on-one sessions, group coaching, and personal appearances at various conferences and gatherings around the world. I've even formulated my take on adaptive fitness and established a fun and powerful Versatile Wellness Coaching System.

I work with clients worldwide, and it is amazing to help them achieve their fitness and wellness goals despite their limitations.

But this book encompasses more than just my most current coaching expertise.

Combining My Life's Passions for Good – The Pieces Come Together

Since the 1990s, I have been a professional DJ, spinning tunes for many crowds. My passion for music has taken me to various places, from intimate gatherings to larger-than-life events. The art of DJing goes beyond playing tracks—it's about reading the room's energy, creating unforgettable experiences, and bringing people together through the universal language of music.

But music wasn't just a hobby; it was my muse. I immersed myself in songwriting, producing, and rapping, leading to the release of multiple independent albums. These experiences fueled my creativity and taught me the importance of self-expression and embracing my unique voice.

Becoming a motivational speaker was exhilarating as I began spreading awareness about disability, advocating for inclusive fitness, and encouraging resilience and personal empowerment. I expanded my public speaking opportunities, shared my experiences, and inspired others to live healthier, more empowered lives.

Beyond my fitness and personal development, my life has been a celebration of versatility. I have acted and studied improv at the Second City Hollywood, honing my ability to find humor and joy even in challenging situations. I have also participated in Toastmasters, discovering the art of effective communication and connecting with audiences profoundly.

A Multi-Laned Path of Learning and Growth

Each phase of my life has been filled with challenges and triumphs, which have contributed to my identity. I understand resilience, authenticity, and the extreme power of facing adversity head-on.

This chapter isn't about flaunting accolades; it's about sharing the invaluable lessons gleaned from every twist and turn. From DJ booths to live venue stages, from the workout room to the Zoom room, I've honed skills that have shaped my career and enriched my understanding of human connection.

Embracing the #UNBREAKABLE Life

So, that's why listening to me would benefit you. I am a living testament to the power of embracing challenges and unleashing the #UNBREAKABLE soul within. I'm more than just an author, speaker, coach, and DJ; I've stared down limitations, battled doubts, and overhauled them into stepping stones to greatness.

This book offers the pearls of wisdom gleaned throughout my life and practical insights to navigate life's twists and turns. You're not alone in this journey; I'm your guide, cheerleader, and travel buddy on the road to resilience and empowerment.

Let's be #UNBREAKABLE together.

Chapter 1

Your Willingness to Change

It's time to begin your journey to being #UNBREAKABLE. And it all starts with a concept that will be the foundation of the path ahead - the willingness to change.

Imagine being at the entrance of a maze, surrounded by towering walls that obscure the path ahead. The #UNBREAKABLE life you want is at the end of the maze. Each twist and turn represents a challenge, an opportunity, and a chance to discover the depths of your resilience. The only way to get there is to move forward into the unknown. You have to change where you're at in order to get where you need to go, and it all starts with your willingness to change.

The Power of Transformation

Change can be intimidating, no doubt about it. As human beings, we are wired to seek comfort and familiarity. The thought of venturing into the unknown can send shivers down our spine. But let me share a secret with you - the most profound transformations often start with a single step into the unfamiliar.

Life is ever-evolving, and change is an integral part of it. If we resist change, we stagnate. If we embrace it, we thrive. We often wait for a breaking point to change, which we call a 'rock bottom.' But why wait for rock bottom—which means unbearable pain—to initiate change? Let's take the reins of our destiny and shape our lives proactively.

A Personal Wake-Up Call

I was brought face-to-face with the power of my willingness to change. Beyond my disability, I had been struggling with my physical health, ignoring the signs that my body was sending me. I was constantly lethargic, overweight, and in a constant stress mode. Then, one day, unbearable stomach pain forced me to confront the reality of my situation.

I quickly made a doctor's appointment and was hoping to find a quick fix, but fate had other plans. After a general examination and the administration of an EKG (Electrocardiogram), the diagnosis suggested I might have experienced a small heart attack. I think the addition of the descriptor "small" was supposed to lessen the blow, but it didn't. Fear gripped me, and I realized I couldn't ignore my health any longer. This was the wake-up call I needed to embrace.

From Breaking Point to Turning Point

The experience made me question why I had allowed myself to reach such a breaking point (pun intended) before taking action. But it also taught me a valuable lesson—change doesn't have to wait for a catastrophe. It can begin right now by prioritizing our well-being and personal growth.

Since then, I've committed to being more proactive in my life. I refuse to let myself reach a breaking point, and so should you. Life is too precious to waste time waiting for the pain to become unbearable.

Confronting Our Own Worst Enemy

As we change, we must face an intimidating opponent - ourselves. We often underestimate the power of self-criticism and self-doubt. The voice inside our heads can be the most persuasive yet the most harmful.

Think about it. How do you talk to yourself daily? If you're like most people, you're probably your harshest critic. It's time to rewrite the script of your internal dialogue and become your biggest cheerleader.

Flipping the Script: Harnessing Positive Self-Talk

Let's have some fun with this! Grab a pen and paper, and let's do an exercise together. Still not a physical exercise, don't worry. Write down those negative thoughts that hold you back and chip away at your confidence. Be honest and open with yourself. Awareness is the first step to creating the life you want and deserve.

Here comes the best part: cross out those negatives and replace them with positives. Turn "I don't have the courage to (fill in the blank)" into "I have the courage to (fill in the blank)!" Embrace the power of positive affirmations and witness the shift in your mindset.

Unlocking True Willingness to Change

As we travel toward becoming #UNBREAKABLE, it's essential to realize that you are more willing to change than you may think. Our natural inclination toward negativity can be redirected toward positivity. It's all about channeling our energy into uplifting thoughts and actions.

The final step is to let go of your preconceived notions. You don't have to know everything, and that's okay. Embrace the role of a student, be open to new ideas, and be willing to listen. Your growth is limitless, and releasing old thought patterns makes space for new possibilities.

Chapter 2

Struggle Versus Challenge

We often encounter adversity and obstacles that test our resilience and determination throughout life. How we perceive and approach these challenges can significantly impact our ability to overcome them. Understanding the difference between "struggle" and "challenge" and embracing a positive mindset can be the key to unlocking our full potential and achieving our goals.

The Struggle Within

Many of us have experienced moments in life where everything feels like an uphill battle—a constant struggle. Whether we're facing a physical challenge, navigating complex relationships, or dealing with financial hardships, struggles can leave us feeling overwhelmed and defeated. And unfortunately, we inadvertently disempower ourselves when we view our difficulties through the "struggle" lens.

The "struggle" mindset is disheartening because it suggests we are fighting against impossible odds with no clear solution or path forward. It reinforces a sense of helplessness, making it impossible to see any opportunity for growth or change. We are stuck in a maze without exits, endlessly searching for a way out.

The Power of a Challenge

On the flip side, a "challenge" implies an opportunity for growth and development—a puzzle waiting to be solved. When we face challenges, we recognize that there is a path, a solution, and a chance for personal growth. Challenges evoke a positive attitude and a proactive approach to overcoming obstacles.

The key difference lies in the perspective we adopt when faced with difficulties. Challenges offer a clear sense of direction and purpose. Like athletes competing in a sport, we embrace the competition, the opportunities to improve, and the thrill of victory. Challenges encourage us to explore creative solutions and possibilities rather than resigning ourselves to defeat.

Turning Struggles into Challenges

Embracing the power of a positive mindset involves turning struggles into challenges. Here are some strategies to help you navigate this:

- **Awareness**: Recognize when you are caught in a cycle of struggle. Acknowledge your emotions and thoughts without judgment. This self-awareness is the first step toward change.

- **Reframe Language**: Replace phrases like "I'm struggling with X" with "I'm facing a challenge with X." By altering your language, you shift your perspective toward opportunity and growth.

- **Seek Solutions**: Approach challenges as puzzles to solve. Engage in problem-solving techniques, research, and explore different avenues to find solutions.

- **Set Goals**: Break down the challenge into smaller, achievable goals. Celebrate each milestone as you progress toward the ultimate solution.

- **Learn and Adapt**: Embrace a growth mindset, recognizing that you can learn and adapt to new circumstances. Be open to change and alternative approaches.

- **Seek Support**: Surround yourself with a supportive network of friends, family, or mentors who can encourage and guide you.

The Power of Perseverance

Conquering challenges requires perseverance, dedication, and consistency. It's essential to stay committed to your goals and remain focused, even when it gets tough. Understand that challenges might take time to overcome, and setbacks are a natural part of the process.

Turning Challenges into Opportunities

Challenges present us with opportunities for growth, learning, and self-discovery. As we face challenges head-on, we gain valuable insights into our strengths and weaknesses. We learn from our experiences and develop resilience and adaptability.

Changing Your Mindset

To truly embrace challenges, it's crucial to change your mindset. Here are a few methods to do exactly that:

- **Believe in Yourself**: Develop a deep sense of self-belief and confidence in your abilities to tackle challenges and achieve your goals.

- **Embrace the Challenges**: View challenges as part of personal growth and fulfillment rather than obstacles hindering your progress.

- **Celebrate Progress**: Acknowledge and celebrate each milestone achieved on your path to conquering challenges. Remember, every step forward is progress. Relate these to the goals I mentioned earlier.

- **Cultivate Positivity**: Surround yourself with positive influences and practice gratitude. A positive outlook can fuel your determination and resilience.

Life is an experience filled with obstacles. By reframing our mindset and embracing these obstacles as challenges as opposed to struggles, we can see them as opportunities for growth and learning and unlock our true potential. The power of a positive mindset lies in recognizing that challenges offer a path forward and a chance to improve ourselves.

The choice is ours—do we allow struggles to define us, or do we embrace challenges as stepping stones toward personal growth and success? By adopting a proactive, positive, and resilient mindset, we become unstoppable, capable of achieving greatness and living life to its fullest. Face your challenges with courage, determination, and an #UNBREAKABLE belief in yourself.

Chapter 3

Change Your Attitude

Attitude is a powerful force that shapes how we think, feel, and act. It can significantly affect our lives, determining how we approach challenges and interact with others. But let's clear up a common misconception—while attitude is essential, it is not the sole factor that leads to success. It's a crucial puzzle piece, but it's not everything.

Attitude, Competence, and Experience

Our attitude toward something cannot replace competence or experience. Confidence is vital but doesn't automatically compensate for lacking the necessary skills or knowledge. We must rely on more than just a positive attitude to perform a task well. We need to cultivate the skills and expertise required to succeed.

Facing Reality

Changing our attitude won't change the facts or reality of a situation. If someone treats us poorly, merely changing our attitude won't alter the person's behavior. The only way to address such issues is to take action and change the situation or distance ourselves from negativity.

The Role of Personal Growth

Personal growth is essential for progress. Our attitude can impact our willingness to learn and grow, but we need genuine efforts to expand our knowledge and skills to achieve meaningful development. A positive attitude combined with continuous learning is a winning formula for success.

While attitude alone isn't enough, it plays a crucial role in living an #UNBREAKABLE life. It shapes how we perceive the world, handle challenges, and interact with others. Let's explore how we can harness the power of a positive attitude to improve our lives!

Step #1 - Analyze Your Current Attitude

We must first become self-aware and mindful of our thoughts and feelings to improve our attitude. Could you take time to reflect on your attitude in various situations? Are you generally positive or negative? Do you tend to approach challenges with optimism or pessimism? Being honest with ourselves is the first step toward meaningful change.

Step #2 - Desire for Change

Once you recognize areas where your attitude could use improvement, you must genuinely want to change. Remember, this is where it all starts—our willingness to change! Desire is the driving force behind any transformation. If you're determined to cultivate a positive attitude, you're more likely to succeed in changing your thought patterns.

Step #3 – Change Your Thoughts

Our thought habits shape our attitudes. We must work on altering our initial thoughts to develop a positive attitude. When you think negatively, quickly replace those thoughts with positive ones. It might feel unnatural initially, but it will become second nature with practice.

Step #4 - Take Responsibility

Our attitude is entirely within our control. While we can't dictate how others behave, we have complete control over our thoughts and reactions. Embrace this power and take responsibility for your attitude. Train your mind to stay positive, even in challenging situations. Many of the negative situations we experience may not be our fault, but it's always our responsibility to control how we respond to them.

The Power of Positive Attitude

A positive attitude opens doors to learning, growth, and better relationships. When we approach life with optimism, we are more receptive to new experiences and opportunities. Our positive energy becomes infectious, lifting ourselves and those around us.

Seeking Support

Maintaining a positive attitude can be challenging, especially during tough times. Remember, you don't have to go through it alone. Seek support and resources to help you stay on track. At www.tonyjacobsen.com, you'll find a wealth of tools, experiences, and insights to guide you toward an #UNBREAKABLE life.

While attitude is not everything, it is fundamental to living a powerful life. Embrace the power of positive thinking, combined with continuous personal growth, and you'll discover the power to overcome challenges, build stronger relationships, and live an #UNBREAKABLE life.

Take charge of your attitude, change it when necessary, and you'll change your life for the better!

Chapter 4

Embrace Progress, Not Perfection

As I look back on my path to becoming #UNBREAKABLE and scan through the past eight years of coaching others to do the same, I've identified a common mistake that just might be standing in the way of you achieving your goals and living an #UNBREAKABLE life.

I've discovered that we all struggle with it sometimes; it's called perfectionism. But guess what? Perfectionism doesn't exist!

The Perfectionism Paradox

Perfectionism can be a tricky beast to tackle because, on the surface, it seems like an admirable trait. People often say, "I'm a perfectionist, and that's why I always succeed." But let me tell you, there's a dark side to perfectionism that can hold you back and leave you feeling defeated.

The paradox of perfectionism is that while it may push you to strive for excellence, it can also become an unyielding barrier to progress. The fear of making mistakes, the anxiety of not measuring up, and the constant comparison to others create an oppressive atmosphere that prevents you from taking risks and trying new things.

Breaking Free from the Perfection Trap

Many believe we must be perfect to achieve our goals and dreams. We think we need to reach some mythical state of flawlessness to succeed. But striving for perfection is like chasing a mirage. It keeps moving further away as we get closer, and we end up feeling frustrated and discouraged.

Here's the truth: Perfectionism is a trap that keeps us from reaching our true potential. It's time to break free from this mindset and embrace progress, not perfection.

The Perfection Comparison Game

One of the biggest culprits feeding our perfectionism is the constant comparison to others, especially on social media. We see carefully curated images of success and happiness, and we think that's the standard we must meet. But the truth is, those images are only part of the complete story. They are just a fraction of someone's truth.

So, the first step to overcoming perfectionism is to stop comparing yourself to others. Your story is unique; you can't measure your progress against someone else's highlight reel. Instead, use those highlights as motivation and inspiration to focus on your growth, goals, and path to greatness.

Embracing Imperfection as a Strength

Here's the truth: imperfection is not a weakness—it's a strength. Embracing imperfection means embracing your humanity, acknowledging that you are a work in progress, and allowing yourself to grow and evolve.

Think about your favorite athletes, musicians, or artists. Did they become legends because they were perfect from the start? Not by a long shot! They honed their skills through relentless practice, countless failures, and a commitment to progress. They embraced their imperfections, learned from them, and used them as stepping stones toward greatness.

Start Now, Start Imperfect

Another trap we fall into is waiting for the "perfect" moment to start working on our goals. We think we need to have everything figured out before taking action. But here's a secret: the perfect moment doesn't exist. The perfect moment is now.

Yes, you heard me right. Start right now. Start imperfectly. Embrace the messy beginnings, the trial and error, the ups and downs. Every step you take, no matter how small, is progress. And progress is what leads to success.

Practice Makes Progress

We've all heard the saying "practice makes perfect," but I'm here to tell you that's not entirely true. In reality, practice makes progress. You learn, grow, and improve each time you put in the effort. That's the beauty of it.

You'll never get anywhere if you wait for perfection before you start. You'll be stuck waiting forever. But if you embrace the concept of progress over perfection and see each step as a chance to get better, you'll be unstoppable.

As you know, I live with a disability, and for the longest time, I believed I had to be "perfect" to be successful in living healthily. I thought I had to overcome all my limitations before I could achieve my ultimate goal of living a healthy lifestyle.

But then I realized that perfectionism was holding me back. I needed to let go of the idea that I had to be flawless to make a difference. Instead, I focused on progress, taking small daily steps to move closer to my dreams. I found ways to start working out and pushing myself properly to get my body moving.

That shift in mindset changed everything. I embraced my imperfections, my struggles, and my unique experience. I realized that being #UNBREAKABLE isn't about being perfect. It's about being resilient, determined, and authentic.

The Fear of Failure and Its Impact

One of the biggest roadblocks created by perfectionism is the fear of failure. Because we fear making mistakes, we stay within our comfort zones and avoid taking risks. But failure is not the enemy. It's a valuable teacher.

We gain insights, wisdom, and resilience every time we stumble and fall. Failure is not a sign of weakness; it's a badge of courage, showing you were brave enough to try. Take each failure as a lesson learned; you learned what NOT to do next time you try. As the great Michael Jordan said, "Don't be afraid to fail; be afraid not to try."

Embrace The Imperfect Time

It's time to embrace your #UNBREAKABLE imperfections. Let go of the need to be perfect and start celebrating your progress. Remember, there is no perfect version of you that you need to become. You are perfect just as you are, imperfections and all. You have the strength, the resilience, and the courage to break free from the chains of perfectionism and embrace your imperfections.

Remember that progress is the compass that guides you. Each step forward, no matter how small, is a victory. Every stumble and fall is a lesson learned. And with each new day, you can be better than you were yesterday.

Chapter 5

Building Happy and How to Truly Get There

Happiness is the elusive feeling we all crave. But what does it truly mean to be happy? If you read my book, "Disable Your Disability," you'll know that "Middle Happy" is a concept that overtakes our lives but something we can work through to reach 100% happiness. It was a bold stance for me to take, but I stand by it. Be sure to read or re-read that chapter to get familiar with "Middle Happy."

Happiness is about being fully satisfied, finding joy even in tough times, and appreciating every moment. Unfortunately, many of us are stuck in negativity, barely experiencing true happiness. To unlock the magic of happiness, we must shift and embrace life's positive side.

I've focused on three essential steps to living a happier life and would like to share those with you. When you embrace them, you'll reach 100% happiness as well!

Step #1 – Embrace Exercise

Exercise is a powerful tool for boosting happiness. Regardless of your current fitness level, everyone can engage in some form of movement. When you exercise, your body releases two important chemicals: dopamine and serotonin. Dopamine is a quick-hit chemical that brings pleasure, even during challenging workouts. Serotonin provides a longer-lasting sense of pleasure, emotional control, and stability. Additionally, exercise builds confidence in your physical abilities and appearance, enhancing your happiness.

When I was younger, I used to despise exercise. As a person with a disability, I often felt ashamed and frustrated by my body's limitations. I believed that exercise wasn't meant for someone like me. However, I couldn't have been more wrong.

After experiencing my health-related problems at 42 years of age and coming to grips with the fact that I would need to exercise to save my life, I was still skeptical, but I took the leap of faith and started my fitness journey.

Surprisingly, focusing on exercise became a significant turning point in my life. It wasn't easy at first, but as I persisted, I started feeling the dopamine rush after each workout. It was exhilarating! I began to appreciate my body's capabilities and my progress. Over time, my physical health improved, and I also found a new sense of joy and satisfaction in life. Exercise had become a key ingredient in my recipe for happiness.

Step #2 - Cultivate Emotional Intelligence

Emotional intelligence is a crucial aspect of living a happier life. It involves being aware of your emotions and understanding that you can control them rather than letting them control you. By developing emotional intelligence, you can respond to situations thoughtfully and avoid knee-jerk reactions driven purely by emotions. Understanding how negativity affects us empowers us to stay in the happy zone more often.

As I became #UNBREAKABLE, I realized that emotional intelligence was pivotal. Growing up with a disability, I faced numerous challenges and sometimes had to deal with negative attitudes from others. Initially, these encounters would profoundly affect me emotionally, leading to anger and frustration. However, I decided to take a different approach.

I began learning about emotional intelligence and how to manage my emotions effectively. I understood that while I couldn't control what others said or did, I had complete control over how I responded to those situations. With practice, I started responding to negativity with grace and composure. Focusing on positivity and understanding disarmed negativity's power over me.

Emotional intelligence also allowed me to find empathy and compassion even in difficult circumstances. By seeing things from others' perspectives, I could navigate conflicts with understanding and kindness. This mindset shift improved my relationships and brought me a deeper sense of fulfillment and happiness.

Step #3 – Surround Yourself with Happy People

Happiness is contagious; surrounding yourself with happy people can positively influence your happiness. Cultivate friendships and companionships with genuinely happy individuals. At first, it might seem challenging, but remember that achieving greater happiness is a team effort. As you embrace steps #1 and #2, you'll naturally attract and connect with other genuinely happy individuals.

I've been fortunate to meet some incredibly positive and joyful individuals throughout my life. Their infectious enthusiasm and optimism uplifted me during challenging times. Being around such people reminded me that happiness is a choice we make, regardless of life's circumstances. These happy individuals brought joy into my life and taught me valuable lessons about resilience and perseverance. They showed me that a positive outlook and a hopeful heart can make all the difference, no matter our obstacles. Their presence in my life encouraged me to strive for greater happiness and spread positivity to others around me.

Remember, genuine, 100% happiness is within your grasp. By exercising, cultivating emotional intelligence, and surrounding yourself with happy people, you can unlock the magic of living an #UNBREAKABLE life filled with joy, satisfaction, and genuine happiness. So take that leap of faith, embrace the positive changes, and let happiness guide you. The choice is yours, and the power to be truly happy lies within you.

Chapter 6

Consistent Habits for the WIN!

Consistency is the key to living an #UNBREAKABLE life. I'm passionate about this topic because I know how important it is for success. But I understand that building consistent habits can be challenging. So, let me guide you through how to do it in a manageable and natural way.

Change Up Your Style

We often try to change too many things at once, overwhelming ourselves. The key is to change up your style by focusing on one habit at a time. Forget about the grand New Year's resolutions where you promise to overhaul your entire life on January 1st, only to find yourself back where you started on February 1st.

Instead, pick just one habit to build. Choose something relevant to your life that you can truly focus on. This will alleviate the feeling of being overwhelmed and create a solid foundation for building consistent habits.

For me, embracing my disability was a huge, life-changing experience. It required a shift in my mindset and daily routines. Instead of trying to change everything at once, I focused on one small habit each month. I started with daily exercises, committing to 15 minutes of movement each morning. By the end of the first month, this new habit had become ingrained in my daily routine.

Be Specific with the Habit

Specificity is the name of the game. Be specific about what you want to achieve when setting your new habit. Don't just say you want to be healthier; define the exact actions that will lead to a healthier lifestyle. For example, commit to working out three times per week—Mondays, Wednesdays, and Fridays—for one hour each session. Now, that's a clear and specific goal!

Being specific takes the guesswork out of the equation. You won't have to wonder when to work out, how long to exercise, or which days to hit the gym. You'll have all the details laid out, making it easier to follow through.

I learned the power of specificity when embracing my disability to get and stay healthy. I used the S.M.A.R.T.E.R Goals method and focused on making sure I was very clear regarding the S-Specificity. I was very specific with the fact that I wanted to start running. I had never done this, but it was a important goal for me. As soon as I set out to run, everything fell into place, and I ended up running in my first 5K race just ten months into my physical transformation. You can read about this part of my journey in my previous book, "Disable Your Disability: Live the Healthy Life You Deserve!"

From that point on, I have been as specific as possible with every goal I take on, which helps me stay consistent and achieve it faster.

Pair Habits Together

Pairing habits is a powerful way to seamlessly integrate new behaviors into your daily life. Think about habits you already have and do without even thinking. Now, use them as triggers to kickstart your new habits.

For instance, if you already have a daily coffee ritual, you can use it as a pairing tool. If you aim to read the Bible daily, do it right after you pour your cup of coffee. If you want to exercise regularly, schedule your workouts right after your morning coffee. Not only will it make the new habit easier to remember, but it will also act as your pre-workout and enhance your overall experience!

By pairing the new habit with an existing one, you'll create a natural flow that helps the new behavior stick faster.

Soon, you'll find yourself doing it effortlessly, without thinking about it.

Embracing my disability required forming new habits that would support my growth and well-being. I paired my morning exercises with meditation to start my day with a positive and focused mindset. This combination became my foundation for facing challenges with resilience and determination.

Consistency: Your Path to #UNBREAKABLE Living

Consistency isn't just a concept; it's a way of life and the backbone of being #UNBREAKABLE. Adopting these three steps—changing up your style, being specific with your habit, and pairing habits—will pave the way for a consistent and powerful transformation.

Embracing my disability and building consistent habits allowed me to overcome obstacles and achieve what many thought impossible. Although challenging, I learned that success is more than quick fixes or big leaps. It's about the daily choices we make and the actions we take.

Remember, consistency is not about perfection. It's about showing up for yourself every day, even when life gets tough. It's about committing to your growth and well-being, one small step at a time.

Chapter 7

Is the Safety On? Triggers Be Gone!

Triggers - those little buttons that people or situations push, causing us to think negatively and derail our positive mindset. As you become #UNBREAKABLE, it's essential to understand and deal with these triggers effectively. Let's dive into the world of triggers, uncover the most effective ways to conquer them, and flip that safety on!

What are Triggers?

Triggers are the catalysts that ignite a negative thought process within us. They can be people, situations, news, or any external factors that spark an emotional reaction. Triggers are unique to each individual and can vary widely, but they all have one thing in common - they can throw us off course from our #UNBREAKABLE path.

Assess and Accept the Trigger

The first step in conquering triggers is recognizing their existence and acknowledging their impact on our lives. Too often, we ignore or suppress these triggers, believing they will go away on their own. But the truth is, they will only vanish once we confront them head-on.

For instance, I used to be triggered by seeing people who resembled the person who had bullied me in the past. Even a passing resemblance or similarity in their behavior was enough to stir up negative emotions within me. At first, I tried to brush it off, thinking it was just a passing annoyance. But as I continued to encounter such individuals, the trigger became more potent, affecting my mood and confidence.

Understand You Can't Control the Trigger

Once I identified this trigger, the next step was to understand that I couldn't control it. These people and their actions were beyond my influence. Accepting this fact was crucial for me as I became #UNBREAKABLE.

While it wasn't easy to accept that I couldn't control external triggers, I realized I could control my response to them. It wasn't about suppressing the emotions or pretending they didn't exist. It was about acknowledging the trigger's presence, understanding its root, and deciding how to respond positively and powerfully.

Let's Go Inward

Understanding triggers goes beyond the external circumstances; it's about diving inward. This introspection is part of self-development, personal growth, and the path to an #UNBREAKABLE life. It's asking yourself the most profound question: "Why is this triggering me?"

As I worked more on self-discovery, I uncovered the deep-seated wounds from my past bullying experiences. Seeing people who resembled my past bully triggered memories of that painful time, and it made me feel vulnerable and insecure.

Introspection revealed that I still carried unresolved emotions from my past experiences. I had never fully healed from the bullying, and this triggered response was a reminder of the wounds I had yet to address. It was an opportunity to confront and heal those old hurts, empowering me to break free from the trigger's hold.

The Game Plan

Recognizing this allowed me to build a game plan for effectively responding to triggers. Instead of letting the trigger consume me, I responded with self-compassion and understanding. I learned to be kind to myself, reminding myself I had grown and evolved since those painful experiences.

When the trigger arose, I had my positive ritual ready to counter it. I created a list of affirmations to repeat when I encountered someone who reminded me of my past bully. These affirmations reinforced my worth, strength, and resilience. Instead of dwelling on the past, I focused on the present moment and the powerful person I had become.

Moreover, I found strength in talking to a supportive friend or engaging in creative activities that brought me joy. I learned to lean on my support system and express my feelings rather than keep them bottled up.

Respond, Don't React

Understanding the difference between reacting and responding was crucial in handling triggers effectively. Reacting is purely emotional and often leads to adverse outcomes. Responding involves logical thought and self-care, allowing us to approach triggers from a place of power and self-awareness.

By responding thoughtfully, I no longer let the trigger dictate my emotions or actions. Instead, I empowered myself to take control of my responses, reclaiming my emotional well-being.

Embrace Your #UNBREAKABLE Mindset

The journey to an #UNBREAKABLE mindset is not without challenges but within your reach. By acknowledging and accepting triggers, understanding their roots, and having a game plan to respond positively, you can lead a life of resilience, positivity, and growth. Once you know that triggers are external factors beyond your control, you can begin responding thoughtfully rather than reacting emotionally.

Remember, being #UNBREAKABLE is not about never facing triggers but putting the safety on, conquering them, and emerging stronger. Embrace your triggers as opportunities for self-discovery, and watch your life transform into something extraordinary.

Chapter 8

Mind Hack Into Your #UNBREAKABLE Power

It's been said that if you master your mindset, you hold the keys to the castle. And you know what? That's true! I'm a living testament to the incredible power of mindset hacks. I've learned to embrace my disability, my unique challenge in life, and turn it into my greatest strength. So, let's talk about some mindset hacks that will empower you to overcome any setback and live your most powerful, #UNBREAKABLE life!

Hack #1 - Let Go of the Past

The past can hold us captive, replaying old memories and regrets, preventing us from living fully in the present and creating a bright future. But remember, the past is just that - the past. It's already happened, and we can't change it. What we can control is how we respond to it now.

When I was younger, my disability brought with it a series of negative thoughts and self-limiting beliefs. Hearing "be careful" repeatedly throughout my childhood and young adult years made me feel destined to break and fail. It weighed on my mind, holding me back from embracing opportunities and taking risks. Until one day, I made a powerful decision to break free from the chains of my past.

This reared its ugly head when it came time to get physical with my body. I desperately needed to do something to help myself, but "be careful" kept me from moving. I was scared because I felt that either road I traveled was going to end in pain. How's that for a negative thought?

I realized that holding onto the negativity of my past wasn't serving me; it was hindering my growth. So, I decided to rewrite the narrative. I let go of the fear associated with "be careful" and reframed it into a positive mindset focused on taking calculated risks and pushing myself. Instead of dwelling on past failures, I looked forward to future victories.

You can also release the grip of your past and start living in the present. Embrace the lessons it taught you, cherish the memories that made you smile, and learn from your mistakes. But don't allow it to dictate your future. Shift your focus to the possibilities ahead, and you'll be amazed at how liberating it feels.

Hack #2 - Stop Worrying

Worrying is a natural human response but can be detrimental if left unchecked. I used to worry incessantly about money. As a freelancer in the entertainment industry as an actor, video producer, and even DJ, the unpredictability of my income and financial stability was a constant source of anxiety.

But then I had an epiphany - worrying wasn't solving anything; it only magnified my stress. I realized I needed to redirect that energy toward productive actions that would improve my financial situation.

So, I committed to stop worrying and started taking charge of my finances. This was when I finally started educating myself to gain financial literacy. I learned about money management and investing, sought out new opportunities, and remained open to exploring diverse income streams. As a result, my financial situation improved, and I felt more in control of my life.

Remember, worry is an emotion that drains your energy without yielding any positive outcomes. Instead, focus on being proactive and taking constructive steps toward your goals. Your mindset will shift, and you'll feel empowered and self-assured.

Hack #3 - Snip-Snap - Choose Your Crew Wisely

The people we surround ourselves with significantly impact our lives and mindsets. If you spend time with negative, unsupportive individuals, it's challenging to maintain a positive outlook on life. Building a tribe of #UNBREAKABLE people who uplift, inspire, and challenge you is essential for your growth and success.

As I embraced my disability and began living an #UNBREAKABLE life, I realized the importance of my support network. I carefully assessed the people around me and noticed some were not genuinely invested in my well-being. So, I made the tough but necessary decision to distance myself from those who didn't contribute positively to my life.

I sought out individuals who celebrated my wins, encouraged my ambitions, and provided a safe space for me to be my authentic self. Surrounding myself with like-minded, #UNBREAKABLE souls fueled my determination and reminded me that I was never alone.

Look around you and assess the relationships in your life. Are they helping you grow, or are they holding you back? Surround yourself with individuals who inspire, support, and believe in your potential. Also, it's important to reciprocate these actions. Together, you'll form a powerful tribe of #UNBREAKABLE warriors united in the pursuit of greatness.

Hack #4 - Embrace Your Deservability

One of the most common barriers to achieving our dreams is a lack of self-belief and unworthiness. This is particularly true for individuals with disabilities, as society sometimes unconsciously perpetuates the idea that we are limited in our potential.

Recognizing that you are inherently worthy of living a fulfilling and #UNBREAKABLE life, regardless of your challenges, is crucial. I, too, struggled with this belief initially. But through self-reflection and soul-searching, I realized that my disability didn't define my worth; it was just a part of my uniqueness.

When you embrace your deservability, you acknowledge that you have the right to pursue your dreams, experience joy, and thrive. Allow yourself to release any lingering doubts or self-sabotaging thoughts, and welcome in a mindset of abundance and positivity.

Reframing your perspective about your worthiness will be life-changing. Embrace the belief that you deserve happiness, success, and fulfillment. This shift in mindset will empower you to take bold actions and make confident choices.

You have the power within you! Embrace the mindset hacks I've shared - let go of the past, stop worrying, surround yourself with #UNBREAKABLE people, and embrace your deservability.

I am living proof that these mindset hacks work. I turned my disability into my superpower, and I continue to grow stronger every day. Now, it's your turn.

Chapter 9

You're Already #UNBREAKABLE. Embrace It.

I've covered this, but I want to go a little bit deeper into what being #UNBREAKABLE truly means. You might possibly be saying, "I'm still unclear on what being #UNBREAKABLE means, Tony?" Well, let me expand on it to make it clearer.

First and foremost, being #UNBREAKABLE does not mean you will never face challenges or difficulties. It's essential to understand that being #UNBREAKABLE is not about avoiding adversity but how we respond to and grow from those difficult moments. It's not about denying the pain or pretending we're invincible when we encounter hardships. Instead, it's about acknowledging the pain, understanding what it teaches us, and using that knowledge to reinvent ourselves.

As I look back, I can't help but reflect on my childhood dreams of becoming an artist and immersing myself in the music world. But like many dreamers, I was met with skepticism from adults, including my parents, who urged me to have a "plan B" just in case my dreams didn't work out. At the time, I thought it was wise advice, but looking back, I realize that the idea of a plan B was terrible. It planted the seed of doubt in my mind and distracted me from fully committing to my passion.

Fast forward to my adulthood, and life presented me with challenges I never truly anticipated because I was living with a rare, brittle bone disorder. This meant I faced several fractures and physical limitations. In addition to breaking my bones, my spirit could have broken too. But it was through these moments of physical brokenness, I learned the true meaning of being #UNBREAKABLE.

As I embraced my disability and learned to use proper exercise, nutrition, and a shift in mindset, I began living a healthier and happier life. This sparked my journey of self-discovery, eventually leading me to write my book, "Disable Your Disability: Live the Healthy Life You Deserve!" It was a guide that not only helped me but also empowered others with disabilities to overcome their challenges and embrace their #UNBREAKABLE selves.

Through my experiences as an improv actor, a Toastmasters enthusiast, a professional DJ, and a rapper, I discovered that being #UNBREAKABLE wasn't just about physical resilience. It was about cultivating a strong mindset, a positive attitude, and unwavering confidence. My days at The Second City Hollywood, honing my public speaking skills through Toastmasters, and years of spinning records and rapping on stages taught me the power of embracing uncertainty and the joys of improvising and looking for ways to say "Yes, and" (more on this later) to life's opportunities.

When I faced setbacks in my music career and encountered negative voices telling me I couldn't achieve my dreams, I learned to silence those doubts by adopting the #UNBREAKABLE power of "I Get To." I shifted my perspective from "I have to" to "I get to" and realized that every challenge was an opportunity for growth. You'll learn more about this concept later!

Through all of it, I learned there are specific steps to take to embrace our already #UNBREAKABLE existence.

The first step toward being #UNBREAKABLE is recognizing and accepting that you might be broken in certain areas of your life. It could be emotional, spiritual, or mental, but it is essential to be honest with yourself. Don't be afraid to assess your happiness and gratitude in life. Are you completely content and fulfilled, or do you live in "Middle Happy," where you settle for less than true fulfillment?

Acknowledging your brokenness is not a weakness; it's a strength. It takes courage to confront the areas where you need healing and growth. One way to assess this is to ask yourself, "Am I genuinely happy and grateful for everything in my life right now?" Be honest with your answers. It's okay if you're not 100% happy all the time. This is a starting point for self-discovery and healing.

The next crucial step is recognizing that healing takes time, but don't get stuck in the pity party. It's natural to feel down or overwhelmed when you're broken but remember, the road to healing begins the moment you acknowledge your brokenness. Avoid the temptation to numb the pain with temporary solutions like drugs or alcohol; they only provide a fleeting escape and can lead to additional problems. Instead, seek help and support from those who understand what you're going through.

This leads us to the next step: asking for help. Asking for help might be difficult, but it's a vital step in becoming #UNBREAKABLE. There's no shame in seeking guidance or advice from mentors, friends, or professionals who can offer insights and strategies for healing. It's essential to surround yourself with a support system that uplifts and helps you find your inner strength.

Remember, being #UNBREAKABLE is about embracing growth and healing. It's not about avoiding the challenges but learning from them and reinventing yourself with each breakthrough.

Chapter 10

Cancel The Thought of Toxic Positivity

When I first heard "Toxic Positivity," it didn't sit well with me. The idea that we should view positivity as toxic rubbed me the wrong way. But here's the thing: To be genuinely #UNBREAKABLE, we need a relentless surge of positivity. And that's exactly what I want to discuss in this chapter.

I was scrolling through social media one day and came across the term "Toxic Positivity" being thrown around. It was gaining popularity, and I couldn't help but wonder where it came from and what people were trying to convey. As I dug deeper, I noticed that many individuals, especially those within the disability community, were using this term. Now, this intrigued me even more because, as someone with a disability who has learned to embrace life fully, I began to question if I was missing something important.

After further investigation, I understood the concept behind "Toxic Positivity." It's about not recognizing our pain and struggles and being given the silver lining without acknowledging our feelings. It's true; we all want our pain to be seen and validated. We need to know that our emotions are recognized and understood.

But here's where the problem lies. Most people will stay in their negative emotions. If we dwell on negativity without understanding the power of positivity, we get stuck in a never-ending loop of negative emotions. That's not the path to being #UNBREAKABLE. Being #UNBREAKABLE is about facing our challenges head-on, working through our negative feelings, and finding strength in the power of positivity.

Growing up with a disability, I faced numerous challenges and struggles. I understand what it's like not to be seen or heard. At many points, I got stuck in the negativity, feeling sorry for myself and not believing in what I was capable of accomplishing.

But then something shifted within me. I realized that being positive wasn't about denying my struggles but embracing them and finding the strength to overcome them. So, I went down a path of introspection, looking within myself and asking why I felt the way I did.

That introspection led me to an essential realization: I am in control of how I react to every situation in life. Negative things might happen, but I can choose how I respond.

So, I started surrounding myself with the right people who lifted me up and encouraged me to stay positive.

As time passed, especially after my big transformation at 42, my circle of friends became smaller, but it was filled with individuals who had an #UNBREAKABLE soul, just like me. We supported and uplifted each other, always focusing on staying positive and overcoming challenges together.

To be #UNBREAKABLE, you must embrace positivity as a way of life. It's not about denying your struggles or invalidating your feelings. It's about finding the strength to face and work through those challenges with a positive mindset.

So, how do we cancel toxic positivity and embrace the power of positivity?

Step #1 - Introspection and Questioning

When faced with negative situations or emotions, turn inward and ask yourself why you feel the way you do. Understand that it's okay to feel negative emotions, but don't let them consume you.

Are you reacting? Recognize that you can control how you respond to any situation. Remember, we're responding and not reacting!

Step #2 – Talk About Your Emotions

Don't be afraid to express your emotions. Share your struggles and feelings with trusted friends or family.

When you talk about what you're going through, you'll find that people will support and uplift you, helping you move toward a positive mindset.

Step #3 – Surround Yourself with Positivity

Build a circle of friends who have an #UNBREAKABLE outlook on life. Surround yourself with people who encourage and motivate you to stay positive. Avoid those who dwell on negativity and the pity party mindset.

Step #4 – Embrace Positivity as a Way of Life

Understand that positivity isn't about denying struggles but finding strength in the face of challenges. Make positivity a habit, and choose to see the silver linings in difficult situations. Celebrate small victories and focus on progress.

Step #5 - Keep Moving Forward

Remember, being #UNBREAKABLE is an ongoing process. You will encounter obstacles, but the key is to keep moving forward with a positive mindset. Don't let negative situations define you; embrace them as opportunities for growth.

As you cancel toxic positivity and embrace the power of authentic positivity, you'll experience a shift in your life. You'll find that you can overcome challenges with newfound strength and resilience. Positivity will become your default mindset, allowing you to face adversity with unwavering determination.

Embrace positivity as your superpower, and watch as your life becomes bigger and better. Being #UNBREAKABLE isn't about never facing challenges; it's about rising above them with a relentless surge of positivity.

Chapter 11

Get Out of Your Head and Be #UNBREAKABLE

As you start your journey to being #UNBREAKABLE and begin to look inward, you'll find that you'll get stuck in your head too much. It's a natural occurrence because, as humans, that's what we do; we create thoughts! The issues and roadblocks arrive when we lose control over our thoughts. It's like they're in a crowd and each thought does its best to get and keep our attention. They start running and racing like they're in the Indy 500. And then they start inviting additional thoughts to the party that we don't even want there. The result? We're stuck in our heads and not living and thriving.

Being #UNBREAKABLE isn't just about physical strength; it's about exercising and maintaining mental fortitude to overcome challenges and operate at your personal peak performance.

So let me shine a light on these methods to get out of your head and find your #UNBREAKABLE power.

Dump Your Brain on Paper

Our minds can be filled with a million thoughts, racing a million miles a minute, swimming around uncontrollably, and taking up space in our brains. It's like having a computer that's running out of memory. But worry not; we have a simple solution—dump your brain on paper! That's right, old school! Write down everything on your mind—ideas, to-do lists, worries—to free up mental space and think clearer.

I used to struggle with managing my thoughts, especially with my disability of breaking bones easily. I worried about slippery floors and stairs, which made me miss out on many experiences. But once I started jotting down my thoughts and fears, I felt more in control. I embraced adventure and began moving about the world differently, which was an incredible experience. Dumping my brain on paper freed me from unnecessary worries and allowed me to be more present in the moment.

Journaling for Clarity

Journaling is another powerful tool to tap into your #UNBREAKABLE power. Take time each day to write freely, expressing your thoughts and emotions. It's like decluttering your mind and gaining clarity about your feelings and experiences. Through journaling, you may discover patterns in your thoughts and behaviors that lead to personal growth.

I'll never forget how journaling helped me gain clarity during many challenging periods. I've always been a writer, but it wasn't until later in life that I discovered the magic of journaling. As life situations began to take a toll on my mental well-being, I would experience anxiety whenever I was faced with multiple options and couldn't make up my mind. My journal became a safe space to explore my desires, fears, and ambitions. Writing it down helped me see the bigger picture and led me to make life-changing decisions aligned with my true passions.

Go to Know – Defeating Analysis Paralysis

We've all been there - overthinking and analyzing every little detail, unable to make a decision. It's called analysis paralysis. But an #UNBREAKABLE life thrives on action, not overthinking. Embrace the motto "Go to Know" - leap and try new things. You'll only know something once you experience it, so go there! Experience is the best teacher, and you'll gain valuable insights to propel you forward.

When I wanted to start my motivational speaking career, I faced analysis paralysis—so many "what ifs" held me back. I had spoken a few times throughout my life, but nothing structured or anything that would have been considered a motivational talk. So, I still had quite a few questions swirling in my mind. What would I talk about? What events and audiences would I speak in front of? Can I make money from motivational speaking?

But then I reminded myself of "Go to Know." I leaped and joined Toastmasters. In my club, I delivered my first structured talk. The experience was exhilarating, encouraging me to get up in front of any audience I could and give motivational talks. Not only that, it opened doors to many more opportunities. Embracing this mindset changed my life; now, I tackle new challenges fearlessly.

Cancel the Worry Bush

I first heard about the worry bush from Joel Osteen. He's a very popular Pastor and leader of Lakewood Church in Houston, Texas. He delivered a talk about the concept and it stuck with me ever since.

The main point is that worrying about the future is a futile exercise that drains your energy. Instead of planting a "Worry Bush," live in the present and focus on what you can control. Cultivate a positive mindset, courageously tackle challenges, and let go of unnecessary worry.

There was a time when I worried excessively about how my disability might hinder me in social situations. I constantly planted worry bushes, imagining the worst-case scenarios. Guess what happened? Sometimes, the worst-case scenarios happened! This prompted me to head down a negative path every time.

However, one day, I decided to let go of those worries. I embraced the adventure of socializing more often, didn't experience any more worst-case scenarios, and met some incredible people along the way. This experience taught me that worries are just illusions that keep us from truly living.

Embrace the Adventure

Life is an adventure, and each experience shapes who we are. Embrace uncertainty and step out of your comfort zone. If you know me, you know one of my favorite quotes of all time is from Neale Donald Walsch, "Life begins at the end of your comfort zone." The unknown may seem daunting, but it's where you'll discover your true resilience. An #UNBREAKABLE life is forged through life's adventures.

With my fragile bones and the metal rods in my legs, cold weather does a number on my legs and hips. I was born and raised in Los Angeles, so I've never had to endure prolonged or severe cold periods with our privileged sunny SoCal climate. So when my wife and I decided to move to Detroit, Michigan, I felt anxious. I wasn't sure how my bones would handle the extreme change in climate when Winter arrived.

I was entirely in my head about the move before the move! But I knew it was a chance to embrace the adventure. The move was a huge positive change, and I fell in love with the new environment.

Spending time in the snow, all bundled up, of course, has been an exhilarating and freeing experience. I've learned so much about what my body can truly handle.

I realized that stepping into the unknown can lead to extraordinary experiences that expand our #UNBREAKABLE life.

Choose Positivity Over Negativity

If you're going to be in your head, at the bare minimum, choose positivity over negativity. Positivity is a superpower that fuels your #UNBREAKABLE life. Talk positively to yourself at every moment. Consume positive content throughout your day. Choose to see challenges as opportunities for growth. A positive mindset empowers you to face difficulties with courage and perseverance.

As you progress toward becoming #UNBREAKABLE, remember that it's not about completely evading your thoughts; it's about controlling them to empower you to flourish in a world full of possibilities. Embrace this perspective, and you'll unlock your full #UNBREAKABLE power.

Chapter 12

The Power of Five

It's time to explore the incredible Power of Five. This concept alone can potentially revolutionize your productivity, mindset, life, and #UNBREAKABLE path. So, let's get right into it!

The Inner Circle of Five

First up, we have the Power of Five when it comes to your inner circle. It's time to take a good, hard look at the people you surround yourself with. The secret sauce to being #UNBREAKABLE lies in having a tight-knit, supportive, and empowering inner circle. Keep it to five people or less, ensuring you can vet and nurture these relationships.

When I started motivational speaking, I realized the importance of my inner circle. Five people who genuinely supported and uplifted me became my pillars of strength. They celebrated my wins, questioned me constructively, and always had my back. These empowering friendships fueled my #UNBREAKABLE power and took me to new heights in my speaking career.

Step Away for Five Minutes

The Power of Five also applies to handling emotional situations. It's easy to react impulsively when faced with challenges, but take a breath, step back, and give yourself five minutes. Use this time to analyze the situation rationally and let your emotions settle before responding. Mastering this skill will elevate your decision-making and emotional well-being.

I remember receiving an unpleasant message on one of the many social media platforms that made my blood boil. Instead of immediately firing back, which I would have done in the past, I walked away and gave myself five minutes. In that short span, my perspective shifted, and I was able to craft a calm, constructive response. This simple practice has completely changed how I handle conflicts and preserve my #UNBREAKABLE composure.

Five Minutes of Exercise

C'mon, you knew I was going to talk about exercise, right? Even if you didn't expect it in this chapter, here it is! Applying the Power of Five to your daily movement is a power move! Whether dancing, stretching, walking, or navigating your wheelchair around your house or block, moving your body for five minutes can work wonders for your physical and mental well-being.

I make it a habit to take five minutes of dance breaks during my long hours of writing, video editing, or other desk work. It's not always dancing. Sometimes, I walk around the house a bit. These short bursts of movement energize me and boost my creativity and productivity. It's incredible how five minutes of movement can turn your day around and ignite an #UNBREAKABLE spark.

Challenge Yourself with Five New Things

Life can get monotonous, but you have the power to break free from routine. Embrace the Power of Five by challenging yourself to try five new things. Whether you take up a new hobby, explore a different cuisine, or embark on an adventure, these fresh experiences will invigorate your #UNBREAKABLE energy!

Before my physical transformation, I was the guy who chose to be inside as much as possible. I didn't appreciate being outside. After I got healthier and could move in a stronger, more confident way, I used the Power of Five to challenge myself to try five new outdoor activities. From hiking to biking, each adventure pushed me out of my comfort zone and reminded me of my #UNBREAKABLE status. Embracing new experiences fueled my passion for life and strengthened my belief in my limitless potential.

Practice Gratitude for Five Minutes Daily

Lastly, remember the power of gratitude. Take five minutes each day to reflect on your blessings. Gratitude can shift your mindset, cultivate a positive outlook, and propel you toward an #UNBREAKABLE life.

I started keeping a gratitude journal, spending five minutes each evening jotting down things I was thankful for. It became a heartwarming ritual that made me appreciate life's little joys and helped me see the silver linings in challenges. This daily practice fostered #UNBREAKABLE resilience and an attitude of abundance.

The Power of Five is a toolkit to elevate your #UNBREAKABLE game. Surround yourself with an empowering inner circle, give yourself five minutes to respond thoughtfully, exercise for five minutes daily, embrace new experiences, and practice gratitude for five minutes daily. When you infuse these five elements into your life, you'll discover the awesomeness of your #UNBREAKABLE life.

Chapter 13

Neverending Happiness

By now, you know that happiness doesn't have to be a fleeting emotion or as elusive as we think. I've given you the formula to build happiness, and now I want to tell you how to maintain it so it's neverending. We all want to be 100% happy all the time—not just that middle-of-the-road contentment, but full-blown, heart-bursting joy! Do these things to set yourself up for neverending happiness.

Set Meaningful Goals

Happiness starts with setting the right kind of goals for ourselves. We all have personal aspirations, like earning more money or getting healthier, but happy people go beyond themselves. They set goals that connect them with others and positively impact the world.

As a motivational speaker, something I didn't expect opened up. I realized that my happiness multiplied when my goals were not just about personal achievements but about inspiring and uplifting others. Setting goals beyond our boundaries unlocks a new level of happiness and fulfillment.

It happened again after I became a personal trainer and began helping other people with disabilities. I discovered a profound sense of purpose and joy. Connecting with others, sharing their stories, and empowering them to embrace their uniqueness brought a happiness that transcended any personal success. So, ask yourself, what goals can you set that go beyond you, making a difference in the lives of others?

Accentuate the Positive

Happy people have a remarkable ability to accentuate the positive in any situation. Instead of dwelling on the negatives, they seek out the silver lining. It's like viewing life through a lens of hope, where they find a glimmer of light even in the darkest moments.

I think of my time rocking the turntables as a DJ. Sure, there might be moments when things don't go perfectly. A mix may be slightly off, or there may be a technical glitch. But happy listeners focus on the incredible music and the moments that brought them joy. Embracing positivity not only improves your outlook but also has a ripple effect on those around you, spreading happiness like wildfire.

I remember a particular time when a clubgoer approached me after a DJ gig. I felt pretty off that night and wasn't particularly satisfied with my performance or mixes. However, she thanked me for playing her favorite song, which brought back beautiful childhood memories. While I worried about a few minor mix-ups during the set, she was basking in the happiness of nostalgia. That interaction reminded me that, in life, we get to choose which moments we hold onto—the negative ones that weigh us down or the positive ones that uplift us.

Forgive for Inner Peace

This one is massive: forgiveness. Happy people possess the incredible ability to forgive those who have wronged them. Forgiveness is not about forgetting; it's about freeing yourself from the burden of resentment and bitterness. I'm sure you've heard the old adage, but I'll say it again for the people in the back. Holding onto grudges is like drinking poison and expecting the other person to suffer. Instead, forgive and find inner peace.

Forgiving is not always easy, especially when the hurt is deep. However, I learned that holding onto anger only weighed me down. So, I chose to forgive, not for the other person's sake, but for my well-being. And you know what? As I forgave, I began to heal and find happiness again.

There were many times when I faced discrimination due to my disability, and it left me hurt and angry. But as I went on this journey of embracing my disability and #UNBREAKABLE power, I realized that holding onto that bitterness only hindered my growth. So, I decided to forgive those who had wronged me, not excusing their actions but freeing myself from resentment. And as I did, I felt an immense weight lift off my shoulders, leaving me with a newfound sense of peace and happiness.

Do Your Happy Dance!

Happiness is like a beautiful, joyful dance where you move to the rhythm of life. I know, another 'dance' reference. I'm a DJ; I can't help it! Anyway, it's about setting meaningful goals that connect you with others, accentuating the positive even in the face of challenges, and having the courage to forgive. When you embrace this dance, you become an unstoppable force of joy.

As I continue to be #UNBREAKABLE, I've discovered that true happiness lies within each of us. It's not about seeking happiness externally; it's about unlocking the happiness in our hearts.

Also, the dance of happiness isn't just about individual happiness; it's about creating a symphony of joy in the world. As we set uplifting goals, embrace positivity, and forgive, we become a beacon of happiness, spreading our light to others. Like a ripple effect, our happiness touches the lives of those around us, inspiring them to find their joy.

Chapter 14

Breaking Free from Broken Records

I started my DJ career in the 1990s. Back then, we used to play with these 12" vinyl discs called 'records.' Of course, I'm being funny. I'm sure you know, or at least your parents know, what records are! Now and again, the records would get warped, scratched, or even broken. And when they did, it would throw the whole vibe off. They'd sound funny, skip, give off horrendous noise, or not play. This would throw anyone who was listening or dancing to the music off-beat. And going through life off-beat, won't get you far and won't be fun.

Did you know that we play records in our minds all the time? And the same thing that happens to physical records also happens to the records in our minds; sometimes, they break.

I want to talk about those pesky broken records that keep spinning in our minds, playing negative thoughts on repeat. You know what I mean, right? Those thoughts that just won't quit. They keep skipping and skipping, dragging us down.

We all have unique broken records, those nagging thoughts that hold us back, make us doubt ourselves, and prevent us from living the #UNBREAKABLE life we deserve. They can stem from childhood experiences, past failures, or societal expectations. I want to help you break free from these limiting beliefs and empower you to embrace an #UNBREAKABLE mindset.

Turn Down the Volume

Imagine those broken records are playing at full volume in your mind, keeping you stuck in a loop of negativity. The first step to combat them is to turn down the volume. We don't need to crank those negative thoughts to 11! We can regain control over our minds by consciously acknowledging them and reducing their power.

Think about the broken records playing in your life. What are they saying? "I'm not good enough"? "I don't deserve success"? Whatever it may be, catch yourself when those thoughts arise and turn down the volume. Recognize that these thoughts do not define you and are merely remnants of old programming.

For years, I had a broken record playing in my mind, "Be careful, be careful, be careful!" It stemmed from my brittle bone disability. Everyone around me constantly warned me to be cautious. But this broken record kept me from fully embracing physical activities and living life.

When I recognized the negative impact of this record, I decided to turn down the volume. I challenged it by seeking new perspectives from others, and that's when things began to change. I discovered I didn't have to be bound by that broken record. So, start turning down the volume on those broken records holding you back!

Share Your Broken Records

It may feel daunting, but sharing your broken records with others can be incredibly liberating. Opening up about your struggles allows you to gain fresh perspectives and support from those around you. Remember, sharing is caring, and it's okay to let others in on what's going on in your mind.

We often fear burdening others with our negative thoughts or insecurities. But sharing our vulnerabilities is a powerful way to connect with others and strengthen our bonds. When you let others in, you allow them to offer their insights, guidance, and encouragement.

When I shared my "be careful" broken record with others, it initially felt embarrassing. But it was crucial to my growth. Friends and loved ones offered new insights and encouraged me to reprogram that record into something positive.Their support empowered me to move forward and embrace a more #UNBREAKABLE mindset.

So, find someone you trust and share your broken records with them. You might be surprised at the profound impact it can have on your path to freedom from negativity.

Upgrade Your Mental Equipment

Like a DJ's turntable, our minds need the right equipment to handle the records we play. If your mental equipment is outdated, it might distort the records, making them sound worse than they are. Upgrading your mental equipment means nurturing your mind and keeping it healthy and resilient.

Self-care, mindfulness practices, and meditation are powerful tools for strengthening mental health. They help you build resilience, maintain focus, and gain clarity in challenging times. By investing in your mental well-being, you empower yourself to handle life's challenges.

Stack Up and Play New Records

Take on the challenge of eliminating those broken records that hold you back. Turn down the volume on negativity, share your struggles with others, and upgrade your mental equipment.

Remember, life is like a DJ mix—filled with ups and downs, slow times, fast times, beats, and breaks. But with an #UNBREAKABLE mindset, we can spin our records of positivity, empowerment, and happiness.

Chapter 15

Building an #UNBREAKABLE Team

Slip on your favorite jersey, grab a piece of paper to write your roster, and prepare to create your dream team. You can imagine a sports team or maybe even assembling a group of your very own superheroes. Whichever you choose, it's all about building a solid squad that will lift you up, challenge you, and help you conquer the world. Let me uncover a few vital characteristics you want in your team members to help you achieve your goals.

You Must Be Open to Advice

Before we get into the details of building your dream team, you must possess one essential quality: being open to advice. You're already pretty far into this book, so I'm sure you are. A true leader doesn't have all the answers. Instead, they are willing to seek guidance from others and test different strategies.

It's not always easy to admit that we don't know everything. It takes humility and a willingness to learn from others. But trust me, embracing this quality will be the first step toward assembling your team.

So, ask yourself, are you ready to take advice, to be humble, and to seek guidance? If your answer is a resounding "yes," then you're primed for building your #UNBREAKABLE team.

Here are the three characteristics you should seek in your team members:

Characteristic #1 – Trust: The Foundation of a Strong Team

The first characteristic you should seek in your team members is trust. This is the foundation upon which an #UNBREAKABLE team is built. You need individuals whom you can trust wholeheartedly.

Imagine this person as your confidant, your partner in crime (although I do not condone crime), and your ultimate supporter. They'll cheer you on when you succeed and lift you up when you stumble. They have your best interests at heart and want to see you thrive.

How do you identify someone you can trust with your dreams and aspirations? Well, think about those in your life whom you've sought advice from before. Whose guidance has led to positive outcomes? That's your clue.

My wife has consistently proven herself as one of the most trustworthy members of my team. Time and time again, when I've taken her advice, the outcome has been greater than I had imagined. I can trust her guidance without a doubt! Her unwavering support and wisdom have been instrumental in my journey toward an #UNBREAKABLE life. It's incredible how much we can achieve when we have someone we can trust on our team.

Characteristic #2 – Diversity: The Power of Differing Perspectives

Let's move on to the second key characteristic of a winning team: diversity. No, I'm not talking about the latest fashion trend or the hottest celebrity couple. I'm talking about diversity in your team's composition.

Your team should be a dynamic mix of personalities and skill sets. Trust me, you don't want a group of "yes" people who will merely agree with your every decision. Embrace diversity and seek individuals with differing ideas and backgrounds.

Why is this so important? A diverse team prevents groupthink, that's when everyone agrees without critically evaluating ideas. Instead, diverse perspectives challenge your thinking and open up new possibilities.

I deliberately sought individuals from various fields and backgrounds when I formed my team. I wanted a mix of personalities that would spark creativity and innovation. And let me tell you, it paid off in spades!

Having a diverse team brought fresh insights and perspectives, leading me to make better-informed decisions and achieve remarkable results. What can happen when you bring together people with different experiences and viewpoints is incredible.

Characteristic #3 – Keep It Small: Quality Over Quantity

I want to address a common misconception about team size. Bigger is not always better when it comes to your team. Keeping it small and focused is the key to #UNBREAKABLE success.

Why? Well, a small, close-knit group allows for easier communication and decision-making. You can quickly get everyone on the same page, and there's less chance of misunderstandings or confusion.

So, how many people should you aim to have on your team? I recommend about five individuals—a perfect balance between diverse opinions and streamlined efficiency.

Throughout my years, I've witnessed the power of an evolving team. At times, I had to make tough decisions and replace team members who weren't meeting expectations. Yes, it was challenging, but each change brought a fresh perspective and renewed energy to our endeavors.

Keeping your team small allows you to be flexible and adapt as your goals and circumstances change. Remember, an #UNBREAKABLE team is not set in stone; it's a dynamic force that evolves alongside your dreams.

Assemble Your #UNBREAKABLE Team

Congratulations! You now have the essential elements for assembling your #UNBREAKABLE team. It's time to take action and bring your dream team to life. But remember, leadership isn't about dictating; it's about empowering your team to shine.

Listen to their ideas, value their contributions, and celebrate their successes. Your team is your secret weapon, support system, and the driving force behind your #UNBREAKABLE life.

Having my rock-solid #UNBREAKABLE team with me, I've soared beyond my wildest imaginings. They've been the wind beneath my wings, cheering me on through the rollercoaster of ups and downs, relentlessly nudging me to surpass my expectations. Side by side, we've faced down challenges, planted our victory flags, and turned broken records into the most empowering anthems you can imagine. It's been a wild ride, and we're just getting started!

Now it's your turn.

John Maxwell said it best, "Teamwork makes the dream work." Surround yourself with trusted allies, embrace diversity, and keep your circle small and dynamic. Together, you'll conquer the world and live an #UNBREAKABLE life to the fullest!

Chapter 16

#UNBREAKABLE Productivity

I love talking about productivity. Over the past ten years, I've been a stickler for efficiency in everything I've worked on. In this chapter, we're diving headfirst into the art of getting things done efficiently. I've got some personal stories to share, and by the end, you'll be armed with practical tips to conquer your to-do list with #UNBREAKABLE power!

Embracing the Challenge of Productivity

Life is a wild ride, isn't it? My wife, Teemaree, and I recently moved into a bigger house, opening up new horizons and endless project possibilities. Now, we're not the kind of people who leave things unfinished for months. That's a recipe for anxiety and frustration. We can't function like that, so embracing the challenge of productivity as it pertains to the new house has given us the power to complete projects quickly and efficiently. Our house is now our home!

Acknowledge and Embrace the Ever-Present To-Do List

Let's face it—the to-do list will never be empty. It's an ongoing, dynamic work in progress, and that's completely fine! Rather than stressing about an overflowing list, embrace the notion that tasks will keep coming. The key is to develop a balanced and efficient approach to tackling them.

We all know that feeling of satisfaction when we tick off an item from our to-do list. It gives us a sense of accomplishment and motivates us to keep going. But here's the thing - as soon as one task is done, two more seem to pop up in its place. It can be daunting, but it's essential to remember that life is full of responsibilities and opportunities.

Before you sleep, jot down the tasks you want to accomplish the next day. This practice helps declutter your mind, making space for a restful night's sleep. Trust me; our brains are like hard drives in a computer - they have a finite capacity. So, get those tasks on paper and sleep like a baby!

I remember a time when I relied solely on my memory to keep track of tasks. However, as my responsibilities increased, I found myself forgetting important things and feeling overwhelmed. That's when I realized the power of writing things down. Whether using a physical notebook or a digital task manager, having a to-do list keeps you organized and focused.

The Power of Prioritization

Now, here comes the tricky part - prioritization. Not all tasks are equal, and understanding which ones deserve your immediate attention is essential. Each day brings unique challenges and opportunities, so it's crucial to choose wisely.

Think of your to-do list as a treasure map. You have limited time, and you want to uncover the most valuable treasures first. By prioritizing tasks, you ensure that you spend your time and energy on things that align with your goals and values.

The Two-to-Three Rule

Review your to-do list every morning and select two to three tasks you can realistically complete during the day. Be honest about the time required for each task and allocate time accordingly. (I'll discuss the Law of 3x later to help with this.) This way, you won't feel overwhelmed, and you'll set yourself up for success.

When I started implementing this rule, I was surprised at how much more I could accomplish. Instead of tackling everything at once, I focused on a handful of daily tasks. This allowed me to give my full attention to each task, resulting in better-quality work and a sense of accomplishment.

Are They YOUR Priorities?

Pause for a moment and look at your to-do list. How many of those tasks genuinely belong to you? You'd be surprised to find out how many items are there because someone else thought they should be. Take control of your list and ensure it aligns with your goals and values.

I used to take on tasks that were not essential to my goals simply because others asked for help or thought I should do them. This left me feeling drained and unfulfilled. Learning to say no and focusing on what truly mattered to me was a game-changer. Prioritizing your goals will give you a renewed sense of purpose and energy.

As a team with my wife, we often share tasks around the house. Some are crucial to her, while others are more important to me. Understanding each other's priorities creates harmony and a sense of achievement together.

One day, my wife had a critical work deadline, and I knew she needed uninterrupted time to focus. So, I took over her household chores and responsibilities for that day. It allowed her to concentrate on her work without worrying about the other tasks. In return, she has done the same for me when I had tight deadlines for my creative projects. Supporting each other's priorities and working together as a team allows us to get more done and reach our goals faster.

It's Okay to Say "Not Now"

Remember, you can't do everything at once. Saying "not now" doesn't mean saying "never." It's about realizing that some tasks might not fit into your current timeline. Don't spread yourself too thin; focus on what matters most.

Harnessing the Power of Focus

Distractions are everywhere, and they can derail even the most productive person. To stay on track, you need laser-like focus and a few productivity tricks.

Have you ever heard of the Pomodoro Technique? It's a time management method that involves working in focused intervals (typically 25 minutes) followed by short breaks. This technique boosts productivity, prevents burnout, and keeps you engaged.

When I discovered the Pomodoro Technique, I was skeptical at first. How could taking breaks help me get more done? But as I tried it, I realized the power of focused work. I could maintain peak productivity and avoid mental fatigue. The short breaks gave me time to recharge and refocus for the next interval.

Eliminate Digital Distractions

Technology is a double-edged sword. While it aids productivity, it can also be a black hole of distractions. To stay on course, silence notifications, close unnecessary tabs, and set specific times for checking emails and messages.

It's so easy to get caught up in the digital world. Social media, emails, and notifications can quickly steal your attention and waste valuable time. By setting boundaries and establishing digital-free periods, you can regain control over your time and concentrate on essential tasks.

During my creative pursuits, I discovered that focus is everything. By employing the Pomodoro Technique, I've written books, produced music, and edited videos more efficiently than ever.

One of my proudest moments was completing my first book. Writing a book had always been a dream of mine, but I struggled to find the time and focus to make it happen. Not only did I set up a daily schedule with a block of time dedicated to the book's writing, but I also decided to implement the Pomodoro Technique, and it made all the difference. Within a few months, I had completed my book and achieved a lifelong goal.

I hope you feel a bit more confident now that you're armed with strategies to get things done. Remember, you're crafting your story through the ups and downs, the tasks accomplished, and the goals pursued. With each tick on your to-do list, you're one step closer to realizing your #UNBREAKABLE potential. So conquer your days with purpose and emerge as a productivity rockstar!

Chapter 17

Reboot for an #UNBREAKABLE Life

Have you noticed that your computer or mobile device starts to slow down and feel clunky over time? Well, sometimes our lives can get that way too. But fear not! Just like with tech, we can give our lives a fresh start. It's time to talk about rebooting your sluggish life!

Why Reboot?

Life can be a rollercoaster ride, and we all experience moments when things slow down, crash, break, or take longer than expected. That's when we need a reboot. Think about it like a system refresh—a way to untangle the knots and regain momentum. With all the work I do on my Macbook Pro, rebooting every few days keeps the system running quickly and efficiently. The tech world has taught us the importance of restarting, and we can also apply that lesson to our lives.

Recognizing Patterns

The first step in rebooting your life is to be aware of the patterns you're stuck in. We all have routines, habits, and rituals, some positive and some not. Take a step back and observe your life from the outside. Identify the repetitive behaviors and actions that have become second nature to you.

Self-reflection is essential during this process. Take some quiet time away from distractions and engage in introspection. This is your moment to look inward and unearth the patterns that have become ingrained in your daily routines.

Consider your morning rituals, how you approach work or personal projects, interact with others, and spend your leisure time. Identify both the positive and negative patterns in your life. The positive ones may promote your well-being, but they could still benefit from an occasional refresh.

Back in the day, I worked in an office, corporate America-style, and I followed a daily routine like clockwork: the same drive on my commute, the same coffee shop, the same greetings to my co-workers, the same computer turn-on process. It became very tedious and repetitive, to the point where I felt stagnant and drained of energy. It was time to recognize the pattern, acknowledge it, and make a change. I ultimately quit corporate America and moved into the Entertainment industry.

After working as a creative and performer, it happened again. I realized that I had fallen into a pattern of working in isolation, thinking that solitude would enhance my creativity. However, over time, it felt clunky and stagnant. I rebooted this aspect of my life by seeking new creative collaborations and embracing the energy of bouncing ideas off others.

The Purpose of Patterns

Now, patterns are sometimes good. They often serve a purpose—they help us reach goals and achieve outcomes. But sometimes, we get stuck in these patterns, and that's where the trouble starts. The patterns lock up our productivity and creativity and slow our advancement toward our #UNBREAKABLE life. To reboot successfully, you need to understand each pattern's outcome or goal in your life. Find the finish line of each pattern and be realistic with what the pattern is achieving for you.

Living with our positive patterns, they can quickly become comfortable cages that hold us back from reaching our full potential. Sometimes, we become so accustomed to the familiar that we fear breaking free from it. The fear of the unknown and uncertainty can be daunting, but it's essential to challenge these limitations to live an #UNBREAKABLE life.

For years, I allowed the fear of public speaking to control my life. I was so used to performing as a rapper or DJ that I would avoid opportunities to speak in front of others, believing that people didn't want to hear my personal stories. But then, I realized that this fear was a limiting pattern keeping me from reaching a broader audience and sharing a necessary message. So, I took a leap of faith and embraced public speaking opportunities. It wasn't easy, but it was liberating and allowed me to grow and inspire others.

Interrupting the Patterns

Interrupting patterns is the key to rebooting. Once you've identified them and their associated goals, it's time to interrupt them consciously. However, keep those end goals in mind. You don't want to throw away positive patterns entirely; you want to find new ways to achieve the same goals. It's like changing up your workout routine to avoid plateauing.

With my workout routine, I was enjoying daily exercise. I would do the same workout program week after week. But then I noticed something. My progress was stalling. I interrupted my routine and started exploring different exercises, workouts, and extended programs. I still aimed to live a healthy lifestyle but needed to switch things up to continue growing and progressing.

Once you've identified your patterns and limitations, it's time to embrace change. Remember, change is an opportunity for transformation. But don't try to change everything at once; instead, start with minor interruptions.

Interrupting patterns doesn't mean abandoning your goals or values; it means finding new and refreshing ways to achieve them. Feel free to explore new hobbies, try different approaches, or change your environment. Sometimes, a simple change of scenery can ignite creativity and inspiration.

Facing Resistance and Overcoming Obstacles

As you begin rebooting, you may face resistance—both from within yourself and from others. Change can be uncomfortable, and it's common to experience self-doubt or external pressure to maintain the status quo.

Remember that facing obstacles is a natural part of growth. Embrace them as opportunities to learn, adapt, and develop resilience. Surround yourself with supportive individuals who believe in your ability to live an #UNBREAKABLE life and will cheer you on as you embrace change.

In my own life, my disability caused me to face adversity. There were times when I felt discouraged and doubted my potential. But through self-empowerment, the support of loved ones, and having a handful of day-one road dogs by my side, I learned to embrace my disability as a strength rather than a limitation. This change in perspective allowed me to discover new opportunities and live a life beyond what I once thought possible.

Remember not to worry about what others think as you reboot your life. The expectations of those around us influence some patterns we fall into. But this is *your* life, and *your* happiness matters. Focus on what makes you happy and fulfilled.

Living the Rebooted #UNBREAKABLE Life

As you navigate the process of rebooting your life, maintaining an #UNBREAKABLE mindset is crucial. Be patient with yourself, as change takes time and dedication. Celebrate your progress, no matter how small, and don't be discouraged by setbacks.

Stay connected to your goals and values, and continually remind yourself why you chose to interrupt patterns in the first place. Embrace flexibility and adaptability, as life is full of twists and turns. Remember that your #UNBREAKABLE life is a journey, not a destination.

I challenge you to embrace the reboot. Be aware of your patterns, recognize their purpose, and consciously interrupt them to make a fresh start. Whether you change your morning or evening rituals, try new hobbies, or pursue different approaches to your goals, rebooting is essential for continuous growth.

Remember, you're in control of your life. Don't let any pattern hold you back or dictate your happiness. Shake things up, interrupt the norms, and reboot your way to an #UNBREAKABLE life!

Chapter 18

Quieting Negative Voices

We all know that negativity can creep into our thoughts, affecting how we perceive the world. But don't you worry, my #UNBREAKABLE buddy, because we can completely change our mindset and squash those negative thoughts with the mighty hammer of positivity!

Let me share a story about my trips to visit my parents. I lived in Los Angeles, and their home was over 100 miles away. The two-hour drive often came with heavy traffic, which could lead to some serious frustrations and anger, especially because I wanted to see my parents as quickly as possible and spend quality time with them.

But my wife and I always made it a positive experience. We cherished the time spent together and enjoyed discussing our plans and ideas, making the ride an adventure rather than a burden. However, upon arriving, my parents would immediately comment on the traffic, emphasizing the negative aspect. Way to kill a good mood! We've all been in similar situations. It's easy to fall into that trap.

The Power of Mindset

The key to quieting negative voices is to change our mindset. We tend to focus on the negative aspects of life because that's what we've learned through society, family, and our experiences. But we don't have to be prisoners to this negative thinking. We are in control of our reality and can create a positive one!

Ask yourself, what kind of reality do you want to create? A negative one filled with pessimism, or a positive one brimming with hope and possibility? It's time to take charge of your thoughts and steer them toward positivity.

Break Free from Extremes

Let's break free from extremes and stop seeing everything in black and white. Life isn't just about perfection or failure; there's a lot of gray area in between. We tend to label anything less than ideal as a failure, but there are better ways to approach life. Embrace the shades of gray and find the silver lining in every situation.

I've faced a few setbacks in my career that left me feeling like a failure, especially in my artistic ventures. It's tough when I release something into the world only to hit a wall or get knocked down because my art is very personal. So, those setbacks hit harder than others. But instead of dwelling on the negatives, I saw it as a learning opportunity. I would head back into the studio or sit in front of my computer and work on something new, taking what I learned from the experience to do something different. Shifting my perspective allowed me to grow and improve, leading to new successes.

Interrupting Negative Interpretations

Another way to quiet those negative voices is to interrupt negative interpretations of communication. In this digital age, text messages and online communication can easily lead to misinterpretations. Languages are filled with nuance, so unless a professional writes an email or text message—and even then, there isn't a guarantee—the meaning behind the words can easily get lost and misinterpreted as negative. Don't jump to negative conclusions based on what others say or don't say. Assume the best, not the worst.

Challenge Your Negative Thoughts

Challenge your negative thoughts and ask yourself if they are valid. Are you jumping to conclusions or making assumptions without evidence? Be mindful of how you interpret signs and communication from others. Give them the benefit of the doubt, just as you would hope others would do for you. Don't hesitate to ask questions to clarify the situation.

Mindfulness and Gratitude

Practicing mindfulness and gratitude can also help quiet negative voices. When you catch yourself slipping into negative thinking, pause and take a moment to focus on the present. Be grateful for the things you have, the people in your life, and the opportunities before you. Shifting your focus to gratitude can refocus your mindset and create a positive outlook.

As a motivational speaker, I faced challenges due to my disability. I knew my story was powerful and needed to be shared. But at times, negative thoughts tried to hold me back. I often second-guessed myself and wondered if my story was unique enough. I asked if anyone would care. I even downplayed my disability in some of my first talks, but they didn't go over as well as expected. I finally chose to embrace my disability story as a strength. People started reacting powerfully to my message. It was the response I needed. This shift in mindset allowed me to inspire others and live an #UNBREAKABLE life beyond any perceived limitations.

Surround Yourself with Positivity

Surround yourself with positive influences and people who uplift you. This concept is repeated over and over, and it bears repeating every single time. Their energy will reinforce your positive mindset, help you stay on track, and quiet negative voices.

The Power of Affirmations

I love to say that I'm a woo-woo dude! So, let the woo-woo get within you!

Affirmations are a powerful tool to overcome negativity. Create positive statements about yourself and repeat them daily. Write them down on paper and put them around the house and office. Type them into your favorite notes app on your devices and set an alarm to remind you to read them throughout the day. Affirmations can rewire your brain, helping you believe in your strength and worthiness.

I used to battle self-doubt and imposter syndrome, especially during my first years as a fitness coach and author. I had never been athletic and was coming out of my transformation. Who was I to coach someone else through what I had been through? And who was I to share my story through my first book? Why would anyone listen to me? But through affirmations, I affirmed my capabilities, and slowly, self-doubt retreated, making room for self-confidence and empowerment. I would remind myself through affirming, "I have a powerful message to share with the world." "I have the experience and expertise to coach others on their fitness journey!" This has worked powerfully in my life, and I know it will work for you too.

Cultivating a Positive Environment

Lastly, create a positive environment that fosters a healthy mindset. Engage in activities that bring you joy, spend time with loved ones and friends who support you, and fill your space with uplifting visuals and messages.

The Ripple Effect of Positivity

When we quiet negative voices, we improve our lives and positively influence those around us. Our mindset and energy create a ripple effect, touching the lives of family, friends, colleagues, and even strangers. By being #UNBREAKABLE and embracing positivity, we inspire others to do the same. Quieting negative voices isn't a one-time task; it's an ongoing practice. Be patient with yourself and celebrate your progress. Remember that you have the power to shape your reality. Embrace positivity, challenge negative thoughts, and surround yourself with goodness.

As you begin to live an #UNBREAKABLE life, know you are not alone. Together, we can conquer negativity, cultivate resilience, and embrace the strength within us. Let's be #UNBREAKABLE, my friend, and quiet those negative voices for good! Remember, you are worthy, capable, and deserving of a life filled with positivity and joy. So go out there and live your #UNBREAKABLE life to the fullest!

Chapter 19

Letting Go of the Past

Ah, the sweet sounds of the past! There's something magical about old-school music that transcends time. Whether I'm getting groovy to disco tunes, jamming out to 80s and New Wave hits, or nodding my head to beats from the golden age of Hip-Hop, I can't help but get lost in the rhythm. Music is more than just a collection of notes; it's a time capsule that preserves our memories and emotions.

While I enjoy playing these nostalgic tracks when I DJ or at random times throughout my week, I remind myself not to get stuck in the past. It's natural to reminisce, and I cherish those moments when memories flood back and take me down memory lane.

However, when reflecting on the past, it's crucial to maintain a healthy balance between recognizing its impact on our present and future, while also avoiding the pitfalls of dwelling too much on our past experiences and letting them dictate our current and future actions and choices.

#1 - You Can't Change the Past

How many of us have wished we could turn back time and redo some of our choices? I know I've been there. Whether we regret a missed opportunity or wish we hadn't made certain mistakes, dwelling on the past can consume us if we're not careful.

But here's the hard truth: the past is unchangeable. No matter how much we replay scenarios or ruminate over past decisions, we can't alter what's already happened. What we can do, however, is learn from our past experiences and use them as stepping stones for personal growth.

In my life, I've faced my fair share of setbacks and made mistakes along the way. I used to let those missteps define me, constantly berating myself for not making the perfect choice or taking a wrong turn. But as I ventured into being #UNBREAKABLE, I realized that dwelling on the past wasn't helping me move forward.

Instead of seeing my mistakes as failures, I saw them as valuable lessons. Those moments of "failure" taught me more about myself than any success ever could. They revealed my strengths and weaknesses, shaping me into the resilient person I am today. So, if there's one thing I've learned, it's this: embrace your mistakes, learn from them, and grow stronger.

#2 – Free Up Mental Space

Imagine your mind as a vast, limitless workspace ready to create and innovate. But here's the catch: that workspace has a limited capacity, just like a hard drive on a computer. If we fill it up with too much information from the past, there won't be enough room for living in the present or planning for the future.

Early in my #UNBREAKABLE journey, I felt overwhelmed by everything new I wanted to create and dealing with issues from my past. I realized that I needed to declutter my mind. I wanted to create a space where new ideas and opportunities could flourish. That's when I decided to release my grip on the past and embrace the power of living in the present.

By freeing up mental space, I could fully immerse myself in the here and now, savor life's joys, and face challenges with a clear mind. As I let go of the past, I felt lighter, as if a weight had been lifted from my shoulders. This newfound space became the fertile ground on which I planted the seeds for an #UNBREAKABLE future.

#3 – Let Go of Regrets

Regrets are like anchors, chaining us to our past and preventing us from moving forward. They gnaw at our minds, whispering tales of what could have been, making us second-guess our choices. But holding on to regrets only robs us of the joy and potential of the present moment.

One of the most significant turning points in my life was when I decided to embrace my disability wholeheartedly. For years, I had denied it while I lived with the consequences it would bring. Even though I wouldn't outwardly talk about it frequently, I subconsciously let it define me and hold me back, feeling like I was always at a disadvantage. But then, I had a revelation - my disability wasn't a limitation; it was a unique part of who I am.

When I stopped dwelling on what I couldn't do and started focusing on what I could do, I tapped into an inner well of strength and resilience. I embraced my disability as a gift, one that allowed me to see the world from a different perspective and profoundly connect with others. In that moment of acceptance, my life of being #UNBREAKABLE truly began.

Let Go, Embrace, and Create

I urge you to cherish the past for what it was - a collection of experiences that shaped you. But don't allow it to hold you back or consume your present. Embrace the present fully and use it as a canvas to create an extraordinary future.

Letting go of the past doesn't mean erasing it from our memories; it means liberating ourselves from its hold on us. Embrace your unique strengths and the path that has led you to this moment. Remember, every step you've taken and experience has brought you here, equipped with the tools to build your #UNBREAKABLE life.

So yes, dance to the music of the past, celebrating the memories and experiences that shaped you. Let it inspire you, but don't linger there for too long. Instead, dance through the present, fully engaged in every beat and rhythm. As you move forward, you'll dance into the #UNBREAKABLE future you rightly deserve!

Chapter 20

The Law of 3x

Time is a relentless force that never stops ticking. As a creative individual with many projects and responsibilities, I've always felt the pressure of needing more time. It's a sentiment shared by many. Throughout my life, I've been fascinated by time management, striving to find ways to make the most of each minute. Especially when it comes to my businesses. However, no matter how hard I tried, a nagging feeling persisted that I couldn't accomplish everything I wanted. However, as I intentionally challenged this idea, I discovered a productivity secret that unlocked a world of possibilities.

The Law of 3x Unveiled

After much soul-searching and experimenting, I stumbled upon what I now call the Law of 3x. This simple yet potent concept can significantly impact our approach to tasks and projects. Here it is; whatever time you think a task will take, multiply it by three to get a more realistic estimate. That's the Law of 3x.

The moment this concept dawned on me, it was like a burst of clarity. I knew I had discovered something game-changing. So, I decided to test it in various aspects of my life. I started meticulously tracking my time, from video editing to writing and everything in between.

To my surprise, the Law of 3x repeatedly proved accurate. Tasks that I believed would take an hour often required three hours of dedicated effort. Initially, it was humbling to realize that my time estimates were far from reality. However, this newfound awareness was also crucial to unlocking my overall productivity.

The Psychology Behind It

Why do we consistently underestimate the time it takes to accomplish tasks? This phenomenon can be attributed to a mix of psychological factors. One aspect is our desire to be efficient and productive, leading us to believe we can finish things quicker than we actually can. Additionally, we overlook the challenges and unforeseen obstacles that can arise during a task.

Moreover, studies and experts in time management have discussed similar concepts. Research has shown that people often suffer from the "planning fallacy," wherein they underestimate the time needed to complete a task due to an optimistic bias.

(https://www.sciencedirect.com/science/article/abs/pii/ S0065260110430014)

Acknowledging this optimistic bias can free us from the frustration of unmet expectations. Accepting that tasks may require more time than initially estimated empowers us to plan more effectively and approach our projects with a clear mind.

I've always felt discomfort when I claimed to be "busy" and remained unaccomplished throughout my days. As I integrated the Law of 3x into my daily life, I noticed a huge shift in my productivity.

In the past, I tried to get everything done as fast as possible, often leaving tasks incomplete and feeling overwhelmed. However, when I changed my approach to a more realistic Law of 3x mindset, I began allocating sufficient time for each task on my to-do list. This allowed me to work at a more manageable pace and ensured that I could complete each task to the best of my ability.

I no longer felt stressed and rushed, but instead felt a sense of accomplishment after completing each task. Additionally, I found that the outcomes were of a higher quality, as I was able to devote my full attention and effort to each task.

Overall, adopting this approach has been beneficial. It has allowed me to work more efficiently, feel less stressed, and achieve a greater sense of satisfaction from my work.

Rather than declaring myself "busy," I proudly proclaim my productivity. I'm no longer a slave to time; I have become its master. My schedule feels more balanced, and I experience a newfound sense of control over my creative pursuits.

Applying the Law of 3x

Applying the Law of 3x is a simple yet powerful practice that elevates productivity. Here's how you can implement it in your life:

#1 - Assess Past Experiences

Reflect on past tasks and projects where you had time expectations. Compare your initial estimates with the actual time it took to complete them. Be honest with yourself, and don't shy away from accepting the discrepancies.

#2 – Adopt a 3x Mindset

Once you grasp the concept's validity, begin adopting a 3x mindset. When planning your tasks, multiply the time you think you'll need by three. Embrace this approach, knowing it will lead to more realistic expectations and reduce stress.

#3 - Time Tracking

Start tracking your time to understand your productivity patterns more accurately. Use tools like time management apps or a simple spreadsheet to monitor how long specific tasks take. This practice can help you refine your estimates and make better-informed decisions.

#4 - Prioritize and Delegate

You might feel or think that every project is important. And maybe they are for you. However, not all tasks require the same level of attention or expertise. Prioritize your activities based on importance and urgency. Delegate tasks that others can handle, allowing you to focus on high-impact projects.

As an artist and a renaissance soul, I thrive on creativity and love diving into diverse projects. However, the Law of 3x revealed that I needed to balance assisting others with pursuing my passions.

By being honest with myself about my time constraints, I learned to set boundaries and dedicate ample time to my projects—like writing this book! Embracing creativity without the weight of unmet expectations allowed me to shine in all of my work.

Mastering productivity is a crucial step in your journey to be #UNBREAKABLE. The Law of 3x has been a game-changer for me, and I hope it also becomes a powerful tool in your arsenal. Embrace a realistic approach to time management, acknowledge the Law of 3x, and empower yourself to make the most of each moment.

You can release your true power and create an extraordinary life through self-awareness, honest assessments, and the willingness to adapt. Step into the role of a time master, and watch your productivity soar as you travel down the #UNBREAKABLE path to success. Remember, it's not about being busy; it's about being productive and living your best, #UNBREAKABLE life!

Chapter 21

Quietly Quit... Complaining!

I want to tackle a common habit that plagues many of us - complaining. You know that person in your life who always seems to find something to complain about, no matter how small or insignificant? Maybe you've caught yourself being that person from time to time. It's time to confront this behavior head-on and learn how to convert complaining into an opportunity for growth and positivity. So, let's dig in and explore the reasons behind complaining, its detrimental effects on our lives, and three actionable steps to quietly quit the complaining game for good!

The Nature of Complaining

We all experience moments of frustration, anger, and disappointment. It's a natural part of being human. However, some of us tend to use complaining as an outlet for these emotions. Why do we complain? The answer is simple - we want to vent our frustrations and seek camaraderie and agreement with our feelings. When we find someone who agrees with our grievances, it makes us feel validated and understood. This validation provides momentary relief and comfort.

Imagine you run into a friend, and the conversation starts with a complaint about the weather, traffic, or a recent unpleasant experience. More often than not, the response is a sympathetic agreement; suddenly, you're connected through a mutual complaint. It's like a secret handshake that unites us in our shared frustrations. But here's the catch - this pattern can trap us in a never-ending cycle of negativity, robbing us of the ability to see the positive aspects of life.

The Pitfalls of Complaining

If we constantly complain, we're missing out on the full spectrum of life's experiences. Our negative outlook closes our eyes to the beauty and opportunities around us. Even when something good happens, we can't fully appreciate it because we're fixated on the negative aspects. This perpetual dissatisfaction hinders personal growth and prevents us from reaching our fullest life.

Imagine this scenario: You're enjoying a beautiful day at the beach, but all you can think about is how hot it is, the sand sticking to your skin, and the loud kids nearby. By focusing on these negative aspects, you miss the opportunity to appreciate the sun's warmth, the soothing sound of the waves, and the joy of spending time with loved ones. Complaining robs us of our present happiness and distracts us from the joyous moments that deserve celebration.

Moreover, the effects of complaining extend beyond ourselves. If we surround ourselves with chronic complainers, it's like inhaling second-hand smoke. We absorb the negativity and find ourselves complaining more, perpetuating the cycle. This toxic environment affects our energy levels, relationships, and overall well-being.

3 Steps to Quietly Quit Complaining

It's time to break free from the grip of complaining and cultivate a more positive and resilient mindset. Here are three actionable steps to help you quit complaining and embrace an #UNBREAKABLE life:

Step #1 - Look at the Bright Side

It's easy to get stuck in the negative spiral, but with conscious effort, we can rewire our brains to focus on the bright side of every situation. You can start by practicing gratitude. Each day, find one thing you're grateful for, no matter how small it may seem. It could be as simple as a warm cup of coffee in the morning, a kind gesture from a friend, or a beautiful sunset. By acknowledging and appreciating these little joys, you create a foundation for positivity.

Embracing gratitude has been a bittersweet process throughout my life. As someone living with a disability, I've faced unique challenges, but focusing on gratitude has helped me find strength and resilience. I celebrate my abilities and opportunities instead of dwelling on what I lack. This shift in perspective has allowed me to pursue my passions, perform on stage and DJ, become a motivational speaker, write my books, and live an #UNBREAKABLE life.

Step #2 – Release Expectations

Often, complaining arises from unmet expectations. We set ourselves up for disappointment by expecting situations and people to align with our desires. The truth is we have no control over anyone or anything other than ourselves. By releasing rigid expectations, we free ourselves from disappointment and frustration.

I vividly recall having high expectations for an event, only to be let down when things didn't go as planned. It was a speaking engagement, and I was told a few hundred people would be in attendance. Unfortunately, the event producers let too many details fall through the cracks, and only a few audience members showed up. Even though I didn't get the chance to speak in front of a large audience that day, something else that was even better happened.

After overcoming my initial upset and frustrations, I gave my presentation—without a microphone—and enjoyed the intimacy of the small group. I was able to connect deeply with everyone there. It was a valuable lesson in letting go and embracing the unpredictability of life. By releasing my rigid expectations, I found joy in the unexpected twists and turns, discovering that sometimes the most memorable moments arise from the unplanned and the unanticipated.

Step #3 - Focus on Solutions

Complaining often revolves around what we don't want or can't do. Instead of getting stuck in this loop, focus on finding solutions. When faced with a challenge, quickly pivot from what you don't want to what you can do to address the situation. This shift in mindset propels you into a problem-solving mode, diminishing the urge to complain.

In my own life, I've experienced the power of turning complaints into action. When confronted with obstacles related to my disability, I channeled my energy into finding creative solutions. When I started focusing on my health and working out in a gym, I was frustrated by not being able to do specific exercises as I saw others doing. A reduced range of motion restricted my body. I had to shift my focus to the movements I could do now, no matter how different they felt or looked. By focusing on what

I could do rather than what I couldn't, I unlocked new opportunities and paths, ultimately increasing my range of motion and building a stronger and more flexible body.

Silence the Complainer Within

Armed with these three steps, you can silence the complainer within and embrace an #UNBREAKABLE life. Remember, change takes time, but the journey is worth it. By taking action to quit complaining, you open the door to a life filled with positivity, resilience, and boundless possibilities.

Chapter 22

Live a "Yes, And" #UNBREAKABLE Lifestyle

Welcome to the next level of living, where we'll explore the power of the "Yes, And" lifestyle. It's not just some vague concept; it's a real and powerful way of thinking that can unlock endless possibilities in your life.

The "Yes, And" Mindset

In life, we often find ourselves at a crossroads, faced with decisions that seem to be either "yes" or "no." This binary thinking limits our options and leaves us feeling confined. But what if I told you there's a way to break free from this binary trap? That's where the magic of "Yes, And" comes in.

You see, "Yes, And" isn't just about saying yes to everything that comes your way without discernment. It's about embracing a mindset of possibility, openness, and creative thinking. It originates from the world of improv, where performers build spontaneous scenes by accepting whatever their scene partner offers and then adding to it, saying "Yes, And."

The Power of "Yes, And" in Improv

I experienced the power of "Yes, And" while studying improv at the Second City, Hollywood. Improv isn't just about cracking jokes; it's about building meaningful scenes with a team, and the foundation of this process is the "Yes, And" principle.

Imagine you're on an improv stage, and your scene partner says, "We're in a spaceship heading to a distant planet." Instead of questioning or shutting it down with a "no," you accept their offer with a "Yes, And" mindset. For example, you might respond, "Yes, And it's a planet known for its magical forests and rare creatures." By accepting and building upon each other's ideas, the scene becomes a collaborative masterpiece, full of surprises and delight.

Applying "Yes, And" to Life

Now, here's the exciting part: we can apply the "Yes, And" concept to our daily lives. Instead of getting stuck in either-or thinking, we can open up a world of possibilities by embracing the "Yes, And" lifestyle. Let's see how this can work in various areas of our lives:

Financial Decisions

You may find yourself torn, just as I have, between purchasing a desired item like a MacBook and investing in a passion like DJ equipment. Instead of choosing one and giving up on the other, say "Yes, And." How can you configure your MacBook purchase to allow room for the DJ equipment? You may opt for a slightly older model or less stacked version of the Macbook or look for a used controller. The possibilities are endless when you adopt a mindset of creative problem-solving.

Travel and Adventures

You dream of taking two exciting vacations, but it seems financially impossible. Enter "Yes, And." Explore creative budgeting and planning methods that allow you to experience both adventures without sacrificing either. You may adjust travel dates, find unique accommodations, or discover hidden gems that fit within your budget.

Career and Personal Growth

When faced with a career opportunity, don't limit yourself to a simple "yes" or "no." Apply "Yes, And" to your professional life by exploring how you can embrace new challenges while maintaining your current role. Can you negotiate flexible work arrangements? Is there room to expand your skill set while still excelling in your current position?

Adopting a "Yes, And" mindset can enhance teamwork and collaboration in professional settings. When working on projects with colleagues, instead of immediately critiquing or rejecting ideas, try saying "Yes, And." This simple shift in attitude fosters an atmosphere of inclusivity and empowers team members to contribute freely, leading to innovative solutions and successful outcomes.

Relationships

In addition to making personal choices, the "Yes, And" mindset can profoundly impact our relationships. When we apply it to our interactions with others, we open up opportunities for deeper connections, empathy, and growth.

In our relationships, we often encounter differing opinions and perspectives. Instead of immediately dismissing or arguing against them, try saying "Yes, And" to gain a deeper understanding. Seek to empathize with the other person's point of view and add to the conversation constructively. This approach fosters an environment of open communication and mutual respect.

In my relationship with Teemaree, we occasionally encounter differing opinions, especially when planning weekend activities. Instead of arguing over which activity to choose, we embrace the "Yes, And" mindset. We listen to each other's ideas, acknowledge the merits of both options, and find creative ways to combine elements of each into a memorable experience. We've gone from beach parties to fine dining all in one day.

The "Yes, And" philosophy can strengthen bonds between friends and family members. When someone shares a dream or idea with you, avoid responding with skepticism or discouragement. Instead, say "Yes, And" to encourage their creativity and inspire collaborative brainstorming. Your support might be the catalyst that helps them turn their vision into reality.

Fully Embrace "Yes, And"

I hope you're feeling the power of "Yes, And" thinking and seeing that it's an essential component of the #UNBREAKABLE lifestyle. You'll live a life filled with creativity, abundance, and joy by saying "yes" to opportunities and adding the "and" to expand possibilities.

Imagine a world where everyone says "Yes, And" to each other's dreams, where conversations are filled with creativity and possibility. By embracing "Yes, And," we create a thriving community of #UNBREAKABLE individuals, uplifting one another on the path to success and fulfillment.

As you navigate life's decisions, remember the magic of "Yes, And." It's not about choosing one path over another; it's about creatively weaving your way through multiple possibilities to create an #UNBREAKABLE life that's uniquely yours.

Chapter 23

Don't Lose Your Dinosaur

I love the movie "Step Brothers". If you've seen it, you probably love it too. If you haven't seen it, stop reading now, watch it, and return to this chapter. Suppose you don't want to take the time to watch it right now. In that case, I'll tell you this without spoiling too much: the movie is a blend of outrageous humor and heartwarming moments that follows the absurd misadventures of two grown men embracing the idea of growing up and finding their place in the world. The movie, which stars Will Ferrell and John C. Reilly, is often up for debate as being better than "Talladega Nights: The Ballad of Ricky Bobby"—but I won't go there because I enjoy both!

One of the key moments from the movie comes when the guys have seemingly grown up and are now living their mature lives. But when chaos ensues, they are pushed by their father—brilliantly played by Richard Jenkins— to "not lose their dinosaur." It's a really fun and heartwarming moment because he's reminiscing about when he would pretend to be a dinosaur as a child and how wonderful it made him feel!

When I heard this, it immediately connected with me, and I've never forgotten this important lesson. Now I want to share it with you in hopes that you'll *never lose your dinosaur*.

Remember those dreams you had as a kid? The ones that brought excitement and joy to your young heart? Perhaps you dreamt of becoming an artist, a musician, or a scientist. But as you grew older, those dreams might have been brushed aside because someone told you to "grow up." That's the worst. Well, it's time to recapture that childlike enthusiasm, embrace your dreams, and be unapologetically you!

Say No to Plan B

As a young dreamer, I always wanted to be an artist and immerse myself in the world of music. But many adults, including my parents, told me to have a "Plan B" if things didn't work out. Looking back, I realize that having a plan B was a terrible idea. It distracts you from fully committing to your dream. So, throw away the plan B mentality and focus all your energy on your main goal.

When I started showing genuine interest and potential in music as a DJ, producer, and rapper, I vividly recall my parents urging me to consider other career options besides music. And to be honest, I followed their advice and enrolled in college. I also secured part-time work while going to school. But deep down, I knew I couldn't ignore my passion. So, I decided to pursue my dreams at the same time. I spent my days working tirelessly at school and my job, and after long hours of that work, I would come home and create music. I would also spend my nights and weekends performing in clubs and various events.

I ran myself into the ground through those years and learned so many lessons about what not to do in all facets of life. Pursuing my dreams while at the same time working on satisfying my parents' need to make sure I was taking care of myself led me to burnout physically, mentally, and emotionally.

I was progressing slowly in both my creative ventures and work life. I couldn't keep my promises. Sleep was minimal, and I never felt like I was running at 100% battery level.

Have you ever felt the sting of this? Wanting and knowing deep down that you're meant for greater, but it doesn't logically make sense, so you subject yourself to what everyone else thinks is right? Working tirelessly on a "Plan B" that isn't even your idea in the first place? We all find ourselves in these predicaments, and the results are always the same; it drains our energy, diminishes our hopes and dreams, and sucks the life right out of us!

Plan B is not an option if you want to fully experience the dreams you desire. Don't reduce the energy needed to achieve your goals by diverting it toward something that might just very well be someone else's ideas, dreams, or perceptions of who you are or who you are meant to be.

After graduating college and working in the medical insurance industry for a few years, I became an office administrator for my good friend's small, family-owned telecommunications company. It was a decent job with good pay, and I would still release and perform music "on the side." But I was never thrilled with my life. I knew there was more to experience, but I needed to figure out how to unlock it. I had spent so many years working on plan B I had lost my zest and vision of dreams.

Reconnect With Your Inner Child

Everything changed for me the day my future wife was hired at the company I was working for. She was a beautiful, vibrant breath of fresh air and a fellow creative who loved music, dancing, and enjoying life! She brought a sense of childlike wonder to everything she did, and I was intrigued beyond belief. We made an immediate connection through our shared love of DJing, and within a few months of becoming an official couple, we quit our job at the company and chose to pursue a full-time music career without a plan B!

This reconnection to my inner child reenergized me and my passion for music!

It's time to revive that childlike wonder within you. Who can you engage with, possibly younger than you, or who has a childlike wonder and exudes positive energy throughout their life? You want to participate in activities with younger people, whether they're family members or friends. Spending time with enthusiastic and creative youngsters will reignite that spark in your soul. Their passion for living their dreams will remind you of the dreams you once held.

As I spent more time with my wife pursuing our dreams in the music industry and progressed in my self-discovery, I realized the importance of surrounding myself with those who brought out the best in me. I would spend time with younger folks and attend events, which led to me pulling from their energy. It was infectious! Their passion inspired me to continue reconnecting with my childhood dreams, and it reminded me every day about my excitement for creativity and music.

We went on to record three albums as Dynamite Jive—the World's Most Unexpected Hip-Hop Duo! The experience and feelings that came with producing, recording, and releasing our music, touring the SouthWest, appearing on television and in magazines, and performing for numerous audiences are an accomplishment that goes unmatched to this day.

I'm very grateful I didn't lose my dinosaur; our music made an incredible impact!

Keep Learning, Always

One of the most effective ways to keep your dreams alive is to keep your mind active by continually learning new things. Learning will keep your brain engaged and enthusiastic about life, whether it's a new skill, technology, or a hobby. Don't let age be a barrier to acquiring knowledge.

In my 40s, I took on three large learning opportunities: improv, public speaking, and personal training—and I did them all at the same time! I studied Improv at the Second City in Hollywood, joined a Toastmasters club, and studied and obtained my certification as a personal trainer all within four years.

Now, you may choose one new hobby or passion, and that's fine, but I wanted to explore a new life of coaching and speaking, so I was in it to win it. I graduated from the Second City Conservatory Program, became the President of my Toastmasters club, and won numerous speech competitions. After getting my coaching certification, I wrote my first book and launched a personal training business to help other people with disabilities!

Always… keep… learning!

Even in my 50s, as I continue to author books, motivate audiences with my talks, or coach people along their journey to getting and staying healthy, I'm committed to learning new things every day. It's like adding colors to an already vibrant canvas, and the satisfaction of acquiring new skills is immeasurable. Learning keeps my passion for life alive. It's like a never-ending adventure that fuels my creative spirit.

Let's Make a Pact

So, let's make a pact – never lose your dinosaur! Embrace your dreams with childlike wonder and determination. Ditch the plan B mentality and focus solely on plan A. Surround yourself with the vibrant energy of youth and be inspired to reinvigorate your zest for life. Keep your brain active and young by continually learning new things.

Remember, we all deserve to live unapologetically #UNBREAKABLE lives, chasing our dreams and making them a reality. So, don't lose your dinosaur. Keep that passion alive, and let's live life to the fullest, with joy and determination, every day!

Chapter 24

Choice Versus Decision

Making choices. Making decisions. You might think they're the same, but let me tell you, they're not! This little secret can revolutionize the way you approach life.

The Power of Choice Over Decision

You stand at a crossroads, faced with a life-altering decision. You might be choosing a career path, making a significant life change, or launching off on an adventure. Whatever it is, it feels like a pivotal moment that could shape your destiny.

In such situations, it's easy to fall into the trap of making decisions based on our past experiences and memories. Our minds naturally gravitate toward what we already know, what we're familiar with, and what we've done before. But here's the thing – when we make a decision, we're often limited by our past. We might be held back by fear, self-doubt, or past failures.

Now, imagine the alternative. Instead of making a decision, you make a choice. Making a choice means tapping into the power of now – the present time. It allows you to break free from the shackles of the past and open yourself up to new possibilities, opportunities, and experiences. When you choose, you let go of preconceived notions and embrace the potential for growth and fulfillment.

Let me share a personal story from my life that highlights the impact of making a choice over a decision. For the longest time, I struggled to lead a healthy lifestyle. I have a disability, and it was easy to use it as an excuse not to take care of myself. I was making decisions based on my past struggles, past failures, and all the negative experiences related to my disability.

But one day, everything changed. I stumbled upon the concept of making choices in the present moment, regardless of my past. Instead of dwelling on what I had been through, I focused on what I wanted for my life at that very moment – a healthy lifestyle filled with vitality and joy. And guess what? That choice transformed my entire life.

Choosing to live a healthy life wasn't easy, but it was worth it. Focusing on the present and making choices aligned with my goals gave me a newfound sense of determination and joy. I realized that my past decisions or limitations didn't define me. The power of choice allowed me to live unapologetically #UNBREAKABLE!

Why Choice Trumps Decision

Now, you might wonder, "Tony, why does making a choice hold more weight than making a decision?" The answer is simple: When you make a choice, you break free from the chains of the past. You give yourself permission to explore the unknown and embrace new experiences.

Imagine you have the choice between vanilla and chocolate ice cream. You've had vanilla countless times before and adore it. However, you've never tried chocolate. If you make a decision, you'll likely stick with what you know and choose vanilla—it's safe and familiar.

But what if you make a choice instead? What if you choose to try chocolate for the first time? Whoa! That moment of courage and curiosity can lead to a revelation. Suddenly, your taste buds are delighted, and you've discovered a whole new level of joy—all because you chose the unknown over the familiar.

Embrace the Power of Now

So, how can you harness the power of making choices in your life? It all starts with embracing the present moment. When faced with decisions, pause and ask yourself, "Am I making this choice based on my past experiences or what

I truly desire right now?" Here are three steps to quickly embrace the power of now.

Step #1 - Pause and Reflect

Take a moment to breathe and reflect on the situation at hand. Recognize if your past is influencing your decision-making process. Acknowledge any fears or doubts that might be clouding your judgment.

Step #2 - Focus on the Present

Bring your attention to the present moment. What would you like right now? How does it align with your dreams and aspirations? Let go of preconceived notions and open your heart and mind to the possibilities.

Step #3 - Be Open to Possibilities

Embrace the unknown and be open to new experiences. Remember, life is full of surprises, and choosing the unexplored path might lead to incredible discoveries. Trust in your ability to adapt and grow, even if the outcome isn't clear.

I can't stress enough how much making choices has changed my life for the better. It's what allowed me to embrace my disability and turn it into a source of strength. By choosing to live authentically and focus on my passion for motivational speaking, writing, and coaching, I found fulfillment beyond my wildest dreams.

Choosing to be #UNBREAKABLE meant breaking free from self-imposed limitations and societal expectations. It meant forging my path, embracing uncertainty, and savoring every moment of this beautiful thing called life.

Remember, you have the power to shape your destiny through your choices. Don't let past decisions dictate your future. Embrace the power of now, choose fearlessly, and let your inner strength shine.

Chapter 25

The Myth of Work-Life Balance

A book dedicated to providing tips on living an #UNBREAKABLE life wouldn't be complete without discussing one of the most debated topics in personal growth: work-life balance. It's one of those buzzwords we hear thrown around all the time, and many of us strive to achieve it.

Does the concept constantly wrestle with your peace of mind, too? You might be sitting at your desk, looking over the day's tasks, but your mind is elsewhere - back home with your family. Or perhaps you're at home, trying to enjoy a quiet dinner, but you're mentally still at work, running through your unfinished to-do list.

If you've nodded along so far, I have something to share that might seem radical: Work-life balance is a cultural myth. Before you raise your eyebrows, let me clarify: The pursuit of a perfect balance between work and life is not only overrated but fundamentally flawed.

The traditional notion of work-life balance paints a picture of an ideal life where personal and professional responsibilities balance on a scale in perfect harmony at all times. But the reality couldn't be further from the truth. Why? Because life, by nature, is seasonal.

The Flaw in the Work-Life Balance Concept

The notion of work-life balance suggests that we should have an equal and harmonious distribution of time and effort between work and personal lives at any moment. But let's be honest – life is not that neat and tidy. There will be times when the scale tips toward work and other times when it leans toward personal life.

When we buy into the work-life balance myth, we set ourselves up for disappointment and self-criticism. We may feel like we're failing at life because we can't achieve this elusive equilibrium. Again, work-life balance, as we traditionally understand it, is fundamentally flawed and unattainable.

Life is Seasonal – It's Not Always 50/50

Imagine a tightrope walker gracefully navigating the high wire. Balance is essential for them to stay upright and move forward. Similarly, many of us strive to achieve a perfect 50/50 balance between work and personal life.

But here's the reality – life is not always 50/50, and that's perfectly okay.

Life is seasonal. There are times when professional responsibilities and aspirations take center stage. During these seasons, we may find ourselves dedicating more time and energy to our careers, and that's completely natural. These moments are about intentionally focusing on our work to achieve our goals.

There are also other seasons when our personal lives take priority. We might need to invest more time in relationships, health, or spirituality. Again, this is normal and essential for our overall well-being and fulfillment.

Embrace the Constant Back-and-Forth

Instead of striving for work-life balance, let's shift our perspective to embrace the constant back-and-forth. Life is ever-evolving, and so is our equilibrium. It's about being intentional and present in whatever season of life we find ourselves in.

When you're at work, focus wholeheartedly on your professional responsibilities and aspirations. Be present in your tasks, invest your energy in meaningful projects, and stay committed to your growth.

On the flip side, give them your full attention and love when you're with your family or engaging in personal activities. Be present, cherish the moments, and create lasting memories.

I've experienced this ever-evolving back and forth in my own life. As a motivational speaker and author, there are times when I'm fully immersed in work, preparing for speaking engagements and writing. During these seasons, I intentionally dedicate my time and energy to my professional goals.

But there are also times when my personal life demands more attention. Spending quality time with my wife, nurturing my relationships, and caring for my health become top priorities. And that's perfectly okay!

I've learned that work-life balance is not about dividing my time equally but how I spend it intentionally. It's about understanding the seasons of life and adapting accordingly. Embracing the ever-evolving balance has allowed me to live unapologetically #UNBREAKABLE.

I want to leave you with this newfound perspective on work-life balance. Embrace the ever-evolving back-and-forth, the ebb and flow, and let go of the pressure to achieve a perfect 50/50 time distribution.

Instead, focus on being intentional with your time and fully present in whatever season of life you find yourself in. Remember, it's about giving your all to your work and personal life when the time is right.

Let go of the work-life balance myth and embrace the back-and-forth. Stay intentional, stay present, and keep navigating your dynamic and #UNBREAKABLE life with grace and determination.

Chapter 26

Two Ways of Looking at Life

Get ready for a topic that's a true cornerstone of life and of my book, Disable Your Disability. It's about exploring the profound impact of our perspectives on life, the lenses through which we view obstacles, and their power to help change our lives.

Two Perspectives, Two Paths

Imagine standing at a crossroads, and before you are two paths, each leading to the same destination. However, you can see the end down one, and it's not quite as clear down the other. That's how life often presents us with two ways of looking at things.

The first perspective is the "Show Me the Money" approach. It's the mindset that says, "I need to see it to believe it." This perspective requires concrete evidence before you can trust in something's existence or believe in its potential. It's like waiting for a clear sign or undeniable proof before taking action or having faith in something.

The second perspective is the "Believe and Receive" mindset. This approach is about having faith, trust, and belief in something before it manifests in your life. You set your intention, visualize your desired outcome, and hold unwavering faith that it will come to fruition. You believe it will happen, and then it does.

I'll be honest; I used to be a "Show Me the Money" guy. I needed evidence, proof, and assurance before believing in something or taking action. When my wife and I started making plans or going to events, I would bombard her with countless questions, needing all the details before feeling comfortable.

But life has a funny way of teaching us powerful lessons. When it came to transforming my physical health and becoming healthier, I couldn't wait for evidence or someone to show me the way. My disability, Osteogenesis Imperfecta, added its own set of challenges, but I knew I needed to get healthier.

So, I made a profound shift in my perspective. I embraced the "Believe and Receive" mindset. Instead of waiting for proof or evidence that I could achieve my health goals, I believed I could. I had faith that, with dedication and effort, I would see positive results later.

Adopting the "Believe and Receive" mindset was a game-changer. It's not easy to break free from a lifetime of conditioned thinking, but it's entirely possible. And it's worth it!

This mindset applies to various aspects of life, not just physical fitness. Think about your goals, dreams, and aspirations. Do you need to see immediate results before believing you can achieve them, or can you hold firm to your belief and let the universe align everything for your success?

Early on my path, I didn't have all the answers or a clear roadmap. But I had faith and intention, and the universe responded in kind.

The Magic of Faith and Alignment

It led me to discover a good friend's incredible transformation and his trainer. The right opportunities and connections aligned to support me and it felt like the universe conspired to help me achieve my goals.

And you know what? The same magic can happen in your life when you embrace the "Believe and Receive" mindset. When you have faith, the universe starts to align things for you, bringing the right people, opportunities, and circumstances into your path.

Living with a Half-Full Glass

Now, let's talk about optimism and positivity. Some people dismiss positivity as "toxic," but trust me, it's a powerful tool. Optimism is all about looking at life with a glass half full, seeing the silver lining in every situation, no matter how challenging.

Maintaining a positive outlook may seem complicated, especially during tough times, but it's essential for living an #UNBREAKABLE life. You'll notice a shift in your daily happiness and confidence when you train yourself to see the positive.

Mastering the "Believe and Receive" Mindset

How do you master the "Believe and Receive" mindset? It takes practice, dedication, and patience. Here are some quick tips to get you started:

- **Set Clear Intentions** – Define your goals and dreams clearly. Picture yourself already achieving them.

- **Visualize Success** – Create mental images of yourself achieving your goals. Feel the emotions associated with your success.

- **Trust in the Process** – Have faith that the universe

is working in your favor. Trust that everything is aligning to support you.

- **Maintain Positivity** – Embrace optimism and see the silver lining in every situation. Believe that challenges are growth opportunities.

- **Take Inspired Action** – Take steps toward your goals, even when you can't see the entire path. The universe will guide you along the way.

- **Practice Patience** – Remember, manifestation takes time. Stay committed to your intentions, and be patient with the process.

The two ways of looking at life—"Show Me the Money" and "Believe and Receive"—offer distinct paths to achieving one's goals and dreams.

As someone who has faced physical obstacles due to a disability, I know the importance of embracing the "Believe and Receive" mindset. With faith and intention, you can achieve incredible things.

Remember, the universe conspires to support your journey when you have unwavering belief and trust in the process. Stay positive, keep your glass half full, and watch the magic unfold.

Chapter 27

Transcend Hustle Culture

We live in a society that glorifies hustle culture – the belief that you must work tirelessly, sacrificing sleep, personal time, and even your well-being to be successful. It's easy to fall into this trap, thinking that the more you hustle and grind, the more successful you'll become.

But let me tell you, my fellow #UNBREAKABLE warriors, this path is neither sustainable nor the key to long-lasting success and fulfillment.

Think about this: You're overworking yourself, staying up late at night to complete projects, taking on numerous tasks to demonstrate your value, and barely getting a few hours of sleep. Although you may experience brief moments of productivity, what is the price you pay?

When you push yourself beyond your limits, your physical and mental health, relationships, and overall well-being suffer.

The Pursuit of Longevity and Success

Transcending the hustle culture doesn't mean abandoning your dreams or ambitions. On the contrary, it's about achieving more by embracing a balanced and sustainable approach. It's about finding your rhythm and aligning your actions with your purpose. Prioritizing your well-being and energy levels prepares you for long-term success and happiness.

Think of it as an endurance race. You wouldn't sprint through the entire race; instead, you'd pace yourself, ensuring you had enough energy to finish strong. The same principle applies to life. Instead of sprinting through each day, take strategic breaks to recharge and refocus.

The Importance of Sleep

Let's talk about sleep – the foundation of energy and productivity. Quality sleep is non-negotiable if you want to be #UNBREAKABLE and perform at your best. Your body needs time to rest, recover, and rejuvenate. When you skimp on sleep, your cognitive abilities suffer, making it difficult to focus and make good choices.

I can relate to this struggle all too well. In my hustle days, when I worked full-time in television production, I thought sleep was expendable and I could work around the clock. I would head to work and spend 8-10 hours as a Producer on a weekly show. Then I would go home and spend another 4-5 hours in my recording studio knocking out songs for the next Dynamite Jive album. I loved both creative ventures, but I soon realized that this lifestyle led to a cycle of fatigue and reduced productivity. Which then led to burnout.

So, make sleep a priority in your life. Create a bedtime routine that promotes relaxation and sets the stage for restful sleep. Turn off electronic devices, practice calming activities like reading or meditation, and aim for a consistent sleep schedule.

The Power of the Power Nap

Now, I know life can be demanding, and getting enough sleep every night might only sometimes be feasible. But don't fret! That's where the power nap comes in.

If you find yourself dragging or struggling to stay focused during the day, consider taking a short nap. Even a 10- or 20-minute power nap can refresh your mind, improve your mood, and boost your energy levels. And the best part? Napping won't leave you feeling groggy or mess up your nighttime sleep.

In my early 20s, I remember taking power naps between getting home from work and heading out to the nightclubs. I was always refreshed and ready to party. But as I got older, I forgot about this refreshing nugget of gold. When I finally reintroduced the power nap into my schedule, I accomplished more in a day and achieved greater success in all my endeavors.

Daydreaming for Energy and Creativity

Now, let's dive into a fun and revitalizing practice – daydreaming! As kids, we used to daydream all the time, letting our imaginations roam free. However, as adults, we often neglect this valuable tool for recharging our energy and sparking creativity.

Daydreaming is like a mental escape, allowing us to explore possibilities and envision our dreams coming to life. It's a chance to pause from the hustle and reconnect with our passions and aspirations. So, let yourself daydream, and don't be afraid to envision the extraordinary life you can live.

Focused Breathing for Clarity

When the hustle becomes overwhelming and stress creeps in, focused breathing can be your calming anchor. Take a few moments each day to sit back, close your eyes, and concentrate on your breath. Inhale deeply through your nose and exhale slowly through your mouth.

This simple mindfulness practice can help you reset your mind, reduce stress, and regain clarity. When you breathe with intention, you create space for positive thoughts and let go of negative energy. It's like hitting the reset button for your mind and body.

Transcending Hustle Culture – The #UNBREAKABLE Way

By now, you're starting to see how transcending hustle culture is the #UNBREAKABLE way to achieve your goals and dreams. It's not about working harder but working smarter, embracing self-care, and recharging your energy.

Remember, this is not a sprint; it's a marathon. Pace yourself, and you'll discover that sustained energy and productivity lead to long-lasting success and #UNBREAKABLE greatness.

Chapter 28

Breaking the Cycle of Self-Sabotage

I've said it before, I'll say it again, and I'll keep saying it: we are our own worst enemy at times. That's why it's of the utmost importance that we discuss a topic crucial for empowerment: self-sabotage. Trust me, we've all been there. You set a goal, commit, and then something within you seemingly rebels against it. It's like a silent, internal battle that leaves you wondering, "Why am I holding myself back?" Let's unravel the mysteries of self-sabotage and arm ourselves with the tools to conquer it.

The Psychology of Self-Sabotage

Let's kick this off by looking into the psychology of self-sabotage. Have you ever heard of "psychological reactance"? It's the classic mind trick our brains play when someone tells us what to do. Instantly, we feel the urge to resist. Think about it – even as kids; we'd say "no" when our parents instructed us. This innate response is like a rebellion against losing our autonomy. It's why we've all had that knee-jerk "I don't wanna" feeling when someone tells us to do something.

Now, here's the kicker—this psychological reaction doesn't just happen when others tell us what to do. Nope, it even rears its head when we make commitments for ourselves. When you decide to start that workout program or commit to healthier eating, your mind can revolt. You might think, "Why should I listen to me? I don't wanna do this anymore!" It's a bizarre dance we all partake in, and it's crucial to recognize it.

Turning the Tables: From "Have To" to "Get To"

So, how do we break this cycle? Well, let's flip the script. Instead of telling yourself you "have to" do something, emphasize that you "get to" do it. It's a slight shift in language, but oh boy, does it make a massive difference. Instead of begrudgingly thinking, "I have to work out," tell yourself, "I get to work out and nurture my body." See the magic here? Suddenly, you're not trapped in an obligation but embracing a choice that empowers you.

I battled this internal resistance when it came time for my physical transformation. As someone with a brittle bone disorder, working out took on a whole new level of complexity. The voice of "I have to" echoed louder in my mind, accompanied by doubts and fears. Oftentimes, I'd stand in front of the gym, grappling with my limitations.

Then, I decided to embrace the "get to" mindset. It was a moment of revelation. Instead of dwelling on what I couldn't do, I celebrated what I could. My workouts shifted from obligatory tasks to empowering rituals. I shifted my focus from the weights I couldn't lift to the ones I could. Every movement became a triumph, every session a celebration of my body's capabilities. The resistance melted away as I recognized the honor of caring for myself.

The "get to" mindset is your secret weapon against self-sabotage. It dismantles knee-jerk resistance and replaces it with a sense of privilege and gratitude. It's like your inner rebel takes a step back and says, "Hey, wait a minute, this is a good thing!" This switch won't happen overnight—it's like training a muscle. But with practice, you'll embrace your commitments with a new enthusiasm.

The Balancing Act: Autonomy and Compliance

Alright, let's take a quick detour to the balance between autonomy and compliance. Just as being overly compliant isn't healthy, being overly resistant isn't either. Striking the balance is key. You don't want to obey everything mindlessly, nor do you want to fight against everything constantly. It's about understanding when to assert your autonomy and when to recognize that certain commitments serve your growth.

Embrace Self-Accountability

Here's another key to beat self-sabotage: accountability. When you involve others in your goals, you create a support system that keeps you on track. If you've committed to working out, tell a friend about it. They'll remind you of your "get to" attitude when your inner rebel acts up. It's harder to bail on something when someone else knows about it.

Cultivating an Attitude of Gratitude

Embracing the power of "I get to" infuses gratitude into our actions. You start to appreciate the opportunities you have and feel a deeper connection to the choices you make.

Think about how many people worldwide would love the opportunity to work out, eat healthier, or read books to improve themselves, but they can't for various reasons. We are incredibly fortunate to have the ability, resources, and freedom to do these things.

When you say, "I get to," you shift your focus from obligation to appreciation. Your actions become acts of self-love, growth, and empowerment. Every commitment becomes an opportunity to take charge of your life and become the best version of yourself.

The Power of "Get To"

Now you understand the sinister workings of self-sabotage and have discovered the ingenious antidote—the "get to" mindset. By shifting our perspective from "have to" to "get to," we disarm that inner resistance and infuse our commitments with positive energy. Remember, it's not just about resisting others; it's about embracing choices that empower you. You must balance autonomy and compliance, allowing growth and support to coexist.

Put it into practice. The next time you feel that familiar rebellion bubbling up, remind yourself of the power of "get to." Embrace your commitments as opportunities to thrive. Through consistent practice and self-accountability, you'll build the resilience to overcome self-sabotage and live an #UNBREAKABLE life.

Chapter 29

Defeating the "I Can't Do It" Syndrome

I'm excited to share this chapter with you. It's a keystone in the foundation of being #UNBREAKABLE. Every time I share it with my coaching clients, breakthroughs happen instantaneously. One of the most common obstacles we face is the dreaded "I can't do it" syndrome. We've all been caught in the cycle of thinking about our limitations rather than our possibilities. It's time to break free from this self-imposed barrier and become #UNBREAKABLE!

Permission to Try Something New

When faced with challenges or new opportunities, it's easy to let the words "I can't do that" dominate our thoughts. But what if we change the narrative? The first step is simple yet powerful—permit yourself to try something new. Be willing to step outside your comfort zone and embrace the unknown.

I think about my life and living with O.I., a condition that could have given me every right to say, "I can't do that." However, I realized I could only truly know my capabilities by giving myself a chance to try. So, I forced myself to break free from the "I can't" mindset.

Dare to Dream and Believe

The power of belief cannot be understated. When we dare to dream and truly believe in our abilities, we open ourselves to a world of opportunities. It's time to shift our mindset from "I can't do that" to "I can try, I can learn, and I can achieve."

Don't be afraid to dream big. Allow yourself to envision the future you desire and the goals you wish to accomplish. Embrace the belief that you are capable of taking steps toward those dreams, no matter how small they may be at first.

The Power of Reframing

As we navigate life's twists and turns, reframing our thoughts and language is crucial. Instead of viewing setbacks as failures, see them as opportunities for growth and learning. Reframing our perspective empowers us to see obstacles as stepping stones to success.

Take a moment to analyze your self-talk. Are you constantly saying, "I can't," or do you catch yourself saying, "I'll give it a try?" Start recognizing when you self-impose these boundaries. Immediately change what you said and repeat it. Change "I can't" to "I can!" By changing our language, we begin to shift our subconscious thoughts and open ourselves to new possibilities.

Focus on What You CAN Do

Instead of fixating on our perceived limitations, let's focus on what we CAN do. It's essential to recognize that certain physical challenges may exist, but that's not the whole picture. Even with disabilities and limitations, there is an abundance of things we can achieve.

Building Resilience through Action

Action is the catalyst for change and growth. It's not enough to dream or set goals; we must take consistent action to achieve them. Each step we take, no matter how small, builds resilience and strengthens our #UNBREAKABLE life.

It's important to remember that progress is not always linear. There will be ups and downs along the way, and that's perfectly normal. Celebrate every victory, no matter how small, and use setbacks as opportunities to learn and grow.

Overcoming Frustration with Two Powerful Steps

Frustration is a natural response when we encounter challenges or limitations. However, it doesn't have to define our journey. To overcome the "I can't do it" syndrome, try these two powerful steps:

Step #1 – Create a List of Your Capabilities

Write down every single thing you CAN do. Capture it on paper, no matter how small or insignificant it may seem. Fill an entire page with your accomplishments, strengths, and abilities. This list is tangible proof of your capabilities.

Keep this list close by—fold it and put it in your pocket. Whenever doubts arise, pull it out and remind yourself of how #UNBREAKABLE you are. As you read through the list, you'll witness the abundance of talents and skills you possess.

Step #2 - Push Your Boundaries

Growth happens when we step outside our comfort zones. Start by challenging the limiting thoughts with a simple shift—instead of saying, "I can't," try saying, "Maybe I'll give it a shot" or "I'll try."

Then, push your boundaries a bit. Take small steps toward new experiences, physical challenges, or personal goals. Surprise yourself with what you can achieve when you break free from the "I can't" mindset.

Overcoming Fear of Failure

Fear of failure is one of the biggest obstacles to trying new things. But here's the truth—failure is not the end; it's merely a stepping stone to success. Embrace failure as a valuable teacher and an opportunity to learn and grow.

Remember that even the most successful people in the world have faced failure. Professionals are simply amateurs who didn't give up! The key is to pick yourself up, dust yourself off, and move forward with determination.

Cultivating a Growth Mindset

A growth mindset is the foundation of being #UNBREAKABLE. Embrace the belief that you can develop and improve your abilities through dedication and hard work. See challenges as opportunities to learn and stretch yourself beyond your comfort zone.

A growth mindset allows you to see possibilities where others see limitations. It enables you to break free from the confines of "I can't do it" and embrace all of the power that is within you.

As we continue this #UNBREAKABLE journey, let's remember that we are not defined by our limitations but by our determined spirit. By permitting ourselves to try new things, focusing on what we can do, and pushing our boundaries, we open ourselves to a life of limitless possibilities.

Embrace your uniqueness, dare to dream, and believe in yourself. Reframe your thoughts, take action, and fearlessly embrace failure as a stepping stone toward growth.

Chapter 30

Reach Into the Grab Bag O' Life

Have you ever attended a party and, as a guest, you received a grab bag? Maybe it was called a gift bag or goodie bag. No matter what you called it, it was filled with items, and you had no idea what was in it! But you loved opening that bag and being surprised by its contents.

And life is the same way!

We're on a grand adventure here, and every day is an opportunity to start working on self-discovery. Most of the time, we don't know what's around the corner. Just like a grab bag filled with surprises, life presents countless opportunities to explore, learn, and grow.

For me, living with Osteogenesis Imperfecta has been an adventure filled with unexpected twists, turns, and breaks. Growing up, I faced numerous challenges and physical limitations that held me back.

But here's the thing: I didn't want my disability to define me or dictate the course of my life. I spent many years of my younger and adult life doing just that: being a victim of the circumstances of my disability. But as I started to change my life, which began with my physical transformation, I consciously embraced every opportunity that came my way, even if it meant stepping outside my comfort zone. I started pushing myself to try new things, to experience life to the fullest, and to see where my #UNBREAKABLE drive could take me.

Let's examine the concept of turning life into a grab bag where experiences and adventures will take you beyond your comfort zone and unlock your #UNBREAKABLE potential.

Discovering the Adventurer Within

Remember, life begins at the end of your comfort zone. I am a true testament to this and cannot stress enough the importance of recognizing your line of comfortability and pushing yourself to jump over it, climb under it, or eliminate it altogether.

It's time to break free from self-imposed limitations and dare to try new things. Embrace the unknown with excitement, for it is in the unknown that we find the magic of #UNBREAKABLE living.

The Influence of Relationships

Our paths are often shaped by the people we meet along the way. Personal growth is accelerated when we surround ourselves with inspiring individuals who encourage us to take chances and seize every moment.

I've been blessed to have come in contact with several individuals who have inspired me. But one in particular changed the game for me. When my wife, Teemaree, came into my life, she opened my world to many new experiences. With her guidance and assuredness, we dove into various ventures, changing careers, engaging in non-profit work, and even creating music as "The World's Most Unexpected Hip Hop Duo!" Dynamite Jive. You can listen to our music on your favorite music streaming platform! Her presence has been a catalyst for me and my #UNBREAKABLE path.

Reconnect with Your Creative Passions

As life progresses, we may inadvertently leave behind creative passions we once cherished. Whether storytelling, painting, drawing, or any other artistic expression, it's time to revisit that grab bag of creativity.

Ask yourself, what creative passion did you have when you were younger that brought you immense joy? Now is the time to dust off those long-forgotten pursuits and breathe life into them again.

Redefining Your Comfort Zone

Stepping outside your comfort zone doesn't require a complete life overhaul. It can be as simple as trying a new hobby, exploring different cuisines, or visiting a new city. Life's grab bag offers an array of opportunities to expand your horizons. It's incredible what can be found beyond the familiar.

Occasionally, there will be significant changes!

Both my wife and I were born and raised Angelenos. We love Los Angeles and Southern California. Even though we had been through some fantastic life-changing experiences together, it was a significant leap of faith when we chose to reach into our grab bag o' life and move to the Midwest. We had moved many times during our relationship, but none were outside the Southern California area. We were leaving behind the familiar and venturing into the unknown. We had to adapt to a very different environment, climate, and culture.

I won't lie; it wasn't easy at first. The cold alone was a shock during the first winter season. This was mainly because my bones were getting acclimated to the weather! We faced other challenges and moments of doubt, but we kept reminding ourselves that we were starting a new adventure—a chapter filled with growth and opportunities. And guess what? It has been incredible. We embraced the drastic change in weather and scenery. From the sweltering heat of California to the snow-covered landscapes of Michigan, each day has brought fresh experiences and new memories.

Cherishing New Experiences

The beauty of life's grab bag is that it never runs out of surprises. Each new experience, big or small, adds richness and depth to our lives. By seeking new experiences, we keep the flame of curiosity and enthusiasm alive. This unquenchable thirst for novelty fuels our growth and pushes us further toward being #UNBREAKABLE.

I remember the first time I experienced Michigan snow after moving to the Midwest. It was magical! The sheer joy of feeling the snowflakes on my skin and watching the landscape dissolve into a winter wonderland filled me with childlike wonder.

Diving into Open-Format Living

As a DJ, I pride myself on the fact that I can blend genres seamlessly. Many people refer to this as being an "Open-Format" DJ. I can blend my favorite old-school Hip Hop joint with a Country classic and then move into a 2000s Pop explosion while keeping the rhythm on beat and the dancefloor moving. And just as I've realized through these DJing experiences, life offers an open format for us to explore. Just as I'm not afraid to pull from the grab bag of available music and embrace life's possibilities, don't be fearful to mix and match different experiences.

While staying true to our core passions, let's venture into new territories. Embrace versatility, and you'll find that life's grab bag holds treasures beyond your wildest imagination.

Your Grab Bag

So, how can you reach into your grab bag of life? Embrace change, step outside your comfort zone, and fearlessly pursue new experiences. Seek the support and inspiration of like-minded individuals who encourage you.

Remember, this journey is not about perfection but about progress and growth. As you navigate life's grab bag, you'll find #UNBREAKABLE moments that shape your destiny.

In the end, it's all about experiencing the richness and diversity that life has to offer. So go ahead, reach into that grab bag, and seize the wonders that await you. Embrace the adventure, embrace the change, and most importantly, embrace your #UNBREAKABLE life.

Chapter 31

Is Your Tool Broken? Fix That First!

When it comes to personal development and becoming #UNBREAKABLE, we often rush in with enthusiasm, guns blazing, trying to fix our problems and improve our lives quickly. But usually, we end up frustrated because we're not seeing the results we want—when we want them. We end up stagnant. Stuck.

An excellent example of this is going to the gym to get fit and healthy. You sign up and start working with excitement. But you quit after a month or get injured two weeks into your routine. What's happening? There are two things we need to look at here. First, you might be using the wrong tool to fix your problem—like trying to build your bicep muscles by running on a treadmill. Secondly, even if you have the right tool, your brain—the most essential tool—might be broken. The thoughts and beliefs guiding your actions could be hindering your progress.

When I chose to improve my health, my brain was running on a mix of fear and self-doubt. No matter how much I exercised, my broken tool (my brain) couldn't guide me effectively toward my goal. I needed to fix it first to achieve the transformation I desired.

So, how do we fix the tool? Let me break it down for you:

Tooling Around With Introspection

Imagine you have a toolbox filled with various tools, each designed for a specific purpose. You won't use a screwdriver to get a nail into a wooden board; you'd use a hammer. The hammer is the master tool to get that nail into the board. But what happens if the hammer is broken? Let's think of our brain as the master tool in our life's toolbox—where all our thoughts, beliefs, and actions originate. When life presents us the nails (challenges), we reach for our master tool (brain) to try to fix things. But what if this master tool is broken or malfunctioning? We won't be able to use it, or any other tool, effectively.

That's where introspection comes in—the first step to fixing the broken tool. Introspection is like shining a light inside yourself, closely examining your thoughts, emotions, and beliefs, and asking the tough questions. Facing our inner demons requires courage and honesty, but it's the only way to uncover the root of our challenges.

For me, the pivotal question was, "Why am I so afraid of getting injured and breaking bones?" As someone living with brittle bones, the fear of fractures was deeply ingrained in me, and rightfully so. Through introspection, I realized that my fear was holding me back from fully embracing life and exploring new possibilities, especially when it came to my health and exercise.

As you dig into self-discovery, be gentle with yourself. Allow yourself the space to feel and process your emotions.

Journaling can be an excellent tool for introspection—it helps you organize your thoughts and feelings, providing clarity and insight into your inner world.

You can also explore therapy and read self-help books like the one you're reading now.

The key is to explore your life, past experiences, and beliefs. Self-awareness is the foundation for fixing the broken tool.

Change Your Words, Change Your World

Our words have immense power—they shape our thoughts and influence our actions. When we constantly tell ourselves, "I can't do this" or "It's too difficult," we're setting ourselves up for failure. Remember, it's like hammering a nail with a broken hammer—it won't get the job done.

To fix the broken tool, we must change our language. Let's highlight what we can do instead of focusing on what we can't do. This simple but profound shift can unlock a world of possibilities.

Changing my words was a game-changer (see what I did there?). I stopped telling myself, "I can't participate in physical activities," and instead focused on what I could do. I embraced proper fitness, learning how my body moves and focusing on ways to push myself safely. Emphasizing our strengths and abilities rewires our brains.

The shift in language rewired my brain—it unleashed a newfound confidence and a willingness to explore my capabilities. Changing your words is like replacing that broken hammer with a brand-new one—it empowers you to accomplish your goals with precision and determination.

Surround Yourself with Positivity

Well-known motivational speaker Jim Rohn said, "You are the average of the five people you spend the most time with." Our environment and the people we surround ourselves with profoundly impact our mindset and outlook on life. So it's extremely important to choose our company wisely.

To fix the broken tool, we must change our surroundings. This might be the most challenging part, but it's also the most crucial.

Surround yourself with positive, supportive individuals who uplift and inspire you. Avoid "Middle Happy" or fake positive people who might drag you down with their complaints. Surround yourself with people who believe you can be #UNBREAKABLE and encourage your growth.

Changing my surroundings was both liberating and challenging. I remember consciously changing my environment when I decided to get healthier. I started hanging out at the gym more, visited health-focused shops, and immersed myself in places where people had good health on their minds. This exposure to positive surroundings fixed my broken tool and helped me embrace a healthier lifestyle.

While changing your surroundings may involve leaving toxic relationships or distancing yourself from negative influences, remember that it's essential for your growth. This process has the potential to be the most difficult as you become #UNBREAKABLE but stay the course!

Surrounding yourself with positive people is like upgrading your toolbox with new, reliable tools—they enable you to build a foundation of strength and resilience.

Fixing the Broken Tool for Life-Long Change

By implementing these three essential steps—introspection, changing your words, and changing your surroundings—you'll begin fixing the broken tool in your life. Your brain will no longer be a barrier but a powerful tool to propel you forward in life.

A key point to remember is that there's no shame in having a broken tool—we all do at some point—but you have the power to fix it and find the greatness within you. Just like a mechanic repairs a broken car to make it run smoothly, you can repair your broken tool and live an #UNBREAKABLE life.

Again, be patient with yourself. Changing old patterns and beliefs takes time and consistent effort. But with each step, you'll notice the positive changes within you, and life will respond with opportunities and new experiences.

So, get to work. Reflect on your life, change your language, and surround yourself with positivity. Doing so will unlock the #UNBREAKABLE life you deserve—one filled with growth, joy, and limitless possibilities. Fix that broken tool, and let the transformation begin! Remember, you are #UNBREAKABLE, and you have the power to create a life beyond your wildest dreams.

Chapter 32

Fueling Your #UNBREAKABLE BODY

There are plenty of tips, tricks, and pieces of advice in this book that focus specifically on mindset. However, I would be remiss not to talk about one of the most important aspects of being #UNBREAKABLE: building and maintaining a healthy body. It's not one or the other; it's both. And the foundation of a healthy body starts with what we feed ourselves. Nutrition has played a key role in my #UNBREAKABLE life, and I want to fill up your plate with some nourishing goodness.

As you can imagine, my physical disability profoundly challenged me in this area. In my book Disable Your Disability, I share my journey to a healthier life, but the tips I'll give you here apply to anyone looking to fix their eating habits and live an #UNBREAKABLE life. So, let's jump right in and explore three game-changing steps to start eating better!

Step #1 – Track Your Food to Gain Consciousness

If you want to eat better, you've got to start by understanding what you're eating. It sounds simple, and it is, and it's going to change the way you look and feel about food! Here's the perfect way to get started. For the next seven days, jot down everything you eat—yes, everything! Start with a blank sheet of paper or a digital note. Write the day of the week at the top. Write the time that you eat the item. Then, write the amount of that item that you ate. Do this for seven whole days! Now, this exercise is not about judging yourself; it's about gaining consciousness around your eating habits.

Once the week is over, sit down with your journal and examine your food choices and eating patterns closely. Are you snacking frequently without even realizing it? Are you consuming larger portions than you thought? This introspection is essential to identifying areas for improvement.

After the initial week of tracking, it's time to step up the game and upgrade the technology. Download an app like My Fitness Pal, which can scan barcodes and track your meals more precisely. This app shows you macronutrients, portion sizes, and calorie counts, giving you a clearer picture of your intake. Even the free versions of these apps allow you to use the basic features, which should be enough to expand your understanding of your food intake.

Step #2 - Embrace Portion Control for a Balanced Plate

Portion control is a key element in maintaining a balanced diet. Once you know your food choices, it's time to learn about serving sizes and portion control. There are various methods to do this, but the important thing is to be aware of how much you're eating.

You can use your hand as a guide—your fist represents a serving of vegetables, your palm a serving of protein, and your thumb a serving of fats. Alternatively, you can invest in portion-control containers designed for specific food groups.

Understanding portion sizes will prevent overeating and ensure you get the right nutrients in the right amounts. Remember, it's not about deprivation; it's about balance and nourishing your body with what it needs.

Step #3 - Cut Out the Bad, Make Room for the Good

Now that you've gathered awareness and embraced portion control, it's time for a pantry purge. Clear out the cabinet holding all those tempting snacks, sweets, and unhealthy treats. Trust me, it's a necessary step to create space for the good stuff!

It might feel extreme to throw away food you've bought, but sometimes, we must make bold moves to jumpstart our healthy lifestyle. By removing the unhealthy temptations, you're setting yourself up for success and reducing the risk of giving in to old habits.

Don't worry; this doesn't mean you'll never enjoy your favorite treats again. Once you've established healthier habits, you can reintroduce them in moderation. But for now, focus on filling your kitchen with wholesome, nourishing foods that support your #UNBREAKABLE goals.

Incorporate Fun and Flavor

As you start eating better, remember that it doesn't have to be boring or restrictive. Embrace creativity and explore new flavors in the kitchen. Healthy eating can be exciting, fun, and delicious!

Experiment with new recipes and find ways to make your favorite dishes healthier. Add more fruits, vegetables, whole grains, lean proteins, and healthy fats to your meals. Don't forget to hydrate—water is your best friend!

To save you the hassle of tracking all your meals, start by planning your weekly menu. This way, you'll have a clear idea of what you're eating each day and can ensure it aligns with your #UNBREAKABLE health goals.

Celebrate Your Progress and Keep Going

Eating better isn't a one-time change; it's a lifelong task to revisit frequently. Celebrate your progress, no matter how small, and keep moving forward. Remember that you are #UNBREAKABLE, and your dedication to a healthier life will yield incredible results.

By tracking your food, embracing portion control, and cutting out the bad, you're setting yourself up for long-term success. Every positive choice you make brings you closer to being #UNBREAKABLE.

So, let's fuel our bodies with the nourishment they deserve. Eating better is not just about what's on your plate; it's about empowering yourself to live a vibrant and #UNBREAKABLE life. You've got this! Keep pushing forward, and the rewards will be nothing short of extraordinary. Let's eat better and conquer life, one bite at a time!

Chapter 33

Igniting Your Daily Spark

Motivation has many different meanings to many different people. We each pick and choose what motivates us to get us going each day, but most of us don't talk about what it takes to get it, keep it, and use it as the spark that ignites our #UNBREAKABLE lifestyle. Let me tell you, motivation is a powerful force, but it's just the beginning of the adventure. We need something more profound to light it up and keep the fire blazing.

Let's go ahead and get right into it. Here are three essential steps to get and stay motivated, ensuring you're on the path to #UNBREAKABLE greatness.

Step #1 –Simplify Your Daily Motivation

Simplicity is your best friend if you want to stay motivated every day. Yes, you have big, audacious goals in mind, and that's amazing! But when it comes to your daily actions, keep it real and straightforward.

Don't overwhelm yourself with complicated tasks. This can turn your life into a circus, and that's the opposite of what we are trying to accomplish. Instead, focus on realistic and achievable steps that align with your larger goal. Remember, Rome wasn't built in a day, and neither will your #UNBREAKABLE empire. Each tiny action you take is a vital piece of the puzzle.

Step #2 – Embrace the Power of Intention

Living with intention is a game-changer! What does it mean? It means making deliberate choices, saying no when necessary, and zeroing in on what truly matters to you. Be the captain of your ship, steering it toward the destination you've set your sights on.

Don't let life's distractions sway you from your course. Stay intentional, keep your eyes on the prize, and let that guiding star lead you to the shores of your #UNBREAKABLE success.

Step #3 – Make It Fun, and You've Already Won

Here comes the magic ingredient! Fun! Yes, fun is a non-negotiable part of your daily motivation. Inject that sense of joy into everything you do, even the tasks that might seem mundane or tedious.

When I began my fitness journey, counting calories felt like an uninspiring chore. But I turned the tables by turning it into a game. I used the My Fitness Pal app and began looking at my daily/weekly/monthly calorie counting as a fun challenge. It became addictive! Before I knew it, I had logged my food for an entire year—365 days of epic tracking!

So, find the joy in everything you do. If something feels like a drag, rethink your approach. Make it a game, find the humor in it, and let that spark of fun fuel your motivation.

Harnessing Your #UNBREAKABLE Motivation

As you continue becoming #UNBREAKABLE, remember that motivation is the spark that ignites your inner fire. It's the daily push that keeps you moving forward. Keep it simple, do it with intention, and make it fun! Let these three things be the guiding light that sustains your momentum toward those big goals in life.

Chapter 34

Breaking Bad Habits

Breaking bad habits is no cakewalk, let me tell you. It's a tough nut to crack, but you've got this, and I've got your back. I've been there and struggled with it, but it's all good—I've cracked the code! Get ready to learn some cool tips on how to break free from those pesky habits that are holding you back.

After doing some interwebs research, I discovered something mind-blowing: about 43% of our daily actions are habitual. Crazy, right? Almost half of our day runs on autopilot, guided by those ingrained habits in our subconscious.

But here's the thing—you're not alone and not to blame. Those bad habits aren't easy to shake off because they've become part of us over time. So, let's toss out the self-blame and embrace compassion. You've got the power to break these habits, and I'd like to show you how.

The #UNBREAKABLE Approach: Shifting the Paradigm

Now, here's an incredible paradigm shift—we're not going to rely solely on willpower to break bad habits. Oh no! Instead, we'll change the game by changing the environment around those habits. You heard that right! Our environment plays a pivotal role in shaping our behaviors, so we'll leverage that to our advantage.

Step #1 – Changing the Environment

Imagine you're trying to kick the habit of snacking on junk food. First, pat yourself on the back for taking the first step—awareness! Now, let's change the environment. Get rid of all junk food in your cabinets because the truth is, if you see it, you'll eat it! Now, here's the secret sauce—don't leave a snacking void. Fill that space with nutritious and delicious alternatives. Your taste buds will thank you!

But wait, there's more to this than your kitchen cabinets. Changing your environment also applies to the people you surround yourself with. Just as unhealthy snacks can sabotage your efforts, so can negative influences. If your social circle revolves around people encouraging unhealthy habits or discouraging your goals, it's time for a change.

Let's say you've decided to adopt a more active lifestyle. You've committed to regular exercise, but your current group of friends prefers sedentary activities. They invite you to binge-watch TV shows every weekend, making sticking to your workout routine challenging. Here's where changing your environment extends to your social life.

It's not about ditching your friends entirely, but creating a space for new, positive influences is essential. Seek out individuals who share your fitness goals or are supportive of your goals. Join a local gym to meet like-minded people. Surrounding yourself with those who uplift and inspire you can make a world of difference.

Remember, you're eliminating negative influences and making room for friendships that align with your aspirations. You're replacing unsupportive dynamics with a network that cheers you on. So, when you find yourself repeating those old bad habits, you'll have a circle of friends there to move you in a new direction. That's the power of changing your environment, both in your kitchen and social life. It's about setting yourself up for success by surrounding yourself with positivity and support.

Doesn't that sound like a genius move on your path to self-improvement?

Step #2 – Make It Enjoyable

Breaking bad habits doesn't have to suck. Let's inject some joy into the process! You can find enjoyable activities that align with your new, healthier habit. It could be a fun workout routine, a flavorful smoothie recipe, or even a soothing yoga session. Making it enjoyable triggers that lovely dopamine in your brain, making you more likely to stick with it.

I remember when I started ditching unhealthy eating habits and counting calories every day. Initially, it felt daunting, but using the app My Fitness Pal turned the process into a thrilling game. I challenged myself to hit my macronutrient targets each day, and I'm telling you, it was so much fun! The joy of conquering my goals outweighed the temporary satisfaction of junk food. That's how you level up your #UNBREAKABLE game!

Step #3 – Repeat and Reinforce

Consistency is the name of the game. We're creatures of habit, so we need to repeat our new behavior repeatedly until it becomes second nature. The burning question is, "How long does it truly take to ingrain a new habit?"

The research on this topic varies, with studies offering different timelines. Some optimistic sources suggest it can happen as swiftly as 14 days (and you know I'm all about being optimistic!), while others are more conservative, extending it to a lengthy 90 days. The reality, however, lies somewhere in between, and my experience as a coach has uncovered the sweet spot—around 60 days, on average.

But here's the thing you must consider: your journey is unique. Habits are deeply personal, and the timeline can vary significantly from one person to another.

So, the key is to step out on this path with patience as your guiding star. Don't rush the process; embrace it as an adventure. Think of it as a canvas where you slowly add strokes of a new, improved version of yourself.

As you do, it's important to celebrate your progress, no matter how incremental. Regardless of how minor it may seem, every step forward is a victory. Think of these small wins as the building blocks of your transformation. When you acknowledge and celebrate them, you're reinforcing your commitment to change.

Let's say you want to adopt a regular exercise routine. Even completing a 10-minute workout in the early stages feels like a monumental achievement. Instead of brushing it off as insignificant, celebrate it. Revel in the fact that you showed up, threw on workout gear, and dedicated those precious 10 minutes to your well-being. Recognizing these mini-milestones keeps your motivation soaring and your commitment unwavering.

Breaking bad habits is unique to each person. The key is to stay focused, repeat your new actions consistently, and trust that your #UNBREAKABLE willpower will carry you through.

Triumph over Temptation

Now that you've got the #UNBREAKABLE approach to breaking bad habits, I want to remind you of one crucial thing—the temptation is just a speed bump on your road to success. It's entirely normal to face challenges and slip-ups along the way. The key is to dust yourself off and keep going.

When trying to break my bad habits, I stumbled a few times, too. But instead of berating myself, I embraced compassion. I knew that change takes time and patience. So, don't be too hard on yourself. You're human, and you're allowed to falter. What truly matters is your unwavering commitment to growth and your #UNBREAKABLE life.

Embrace the Ride

You have the power within you to break free from those bad habits that no longer serve you. By changing the environment, making it enjoyable, and repeating your new behaviors; you'll pave the way to a brighter, healthier, more fulfilling future.

Remember, you're not just breaking bad habits but creating new pathways toward your #UNBREAKABLE life. Embrace the ride, celebrate your victories, and relish the joy of growth. You are #UNBREAKABLE, and nothing can stand in your way.

Chapter 35

Always Tap Into Your Inner Optimist

We are called up to bat every day of our lives. We're inevitably going to get thrown some curveballs. Some days, it feels like the universe conspires against us, and nothing goes according to plan. Yet, during these challenging moments, the benefits of staying positive reveal themselves. Staying positive is like a superpower that'll elevate your life. It's one of the most difficult things to do because our emotions significantly affect our minute-by-minute day. So, let's explore the benefits of being positive and how you can nurture your inner optimist!

The Optimism Quest: Embrace the Positive

Let me take you back to a memorable night right before I was about to go live for my #UNBREAKABLE Mixshow. It's one of those moments etched in my memory. The clock was ticking down. I had a few minutes before showtime and needed to make a final adjustment to a vital piece of studio equipment.

Besides my turntables, mixer, or controller, my headphones play a major role in the show. It's how I hear what I'm playing! I usually hang them around my neck as I maneuver around the studio. Since I had to walk around the table in the studio, I unplugged them from this little box I use to split the audio signal, thinking it was routine.

But then, just as I went to plug them back in, the connector on the box snapped! Panic started to rise, and I checked the clock—I only had 60 seconds left to resolve this colossal technical glitch.

My heart raced, and beads of sweat formed. I felt a surge of panic for about 20 seconds. But then, a realization washed over me. Panicking wouldn't solve anything. Instead, I remembered a fundamental lesson: staying calm and maintaining a positive attitude can work wonders in moments like these.

And indeed, it did.

By keeping that positive mindset, I was free to explore alternatives. In those crucial seconds, I devised a workaround that saved the day and allowed me to rock the show as if nothing had happened. It was a powerful reminder that positivity and a clear mind can turn the tide in the face of adversity.

You might wonder, "Isn't being positive all the time a bit unrealistic?" Well, let's dispel that myth once and for all. Those who claim positivity is toxic have yet to experience the true power of optimism. They're trapped in a cycle of negativity, unable to glimpse the radiance on the other side.

There was another time I'll never forget. I was preparing for a big motivational speaking event. I had practiced my speech countless times and was ready to inspire and empower the audience with a beautiful presentation that I created on my computer. But on the day of the event, my laptop crashed, and I lost all my notes and presentation slides. Needless to say, panic set in, and I could feel the negativity creeping in like a dark cloud.

At that moment, I had a choice—to let frustration and despair take over or to find a solution. I took a deep breath, cleared my mind, and started focusing on the essence of my speech. I turned to pen and paper and began writing down the key points from memory.

Surprisingly, the universe conspired again, but this time in my favor. As I took the stage, I felt more connected to my message than ever before. It was like the mishap had made me dig deeper and deliver an even more powerful speech. That day, I learned the true power of staying positive, even in the face of adversity.

Optimist vs. Pessimist: Choose Your Mindset

At some point, we've all had our moments of pessimism. It's only natural, considering the relentless rivers of negativity around us. But here's the thing—a pessimist focuses on the problems, while an optimist seeks solutions. So, which one are you?

Moving into the realm of optimism and breaking free from negativity's grip can be tough. But it's worth every bit of energy because optimism is a superpower. It's the ability to see the cup as half full and uncover solutions amid challenges.

I was a self-proclaimed pessimist for a long time, always expecting the worst outcome in every situation. But that mindset was draining me of energy and joy. My shift from pessimism to positivity was a remarkable ride, one that gained momentum as I went through my personal transformation and reflected on the resilience I'd developed during my childhood, which was peppered with breaks and mends, all thanks to my constant companion—Osteogenesis Imperfecta.

I did my best to be the energetic child most would expect, but since I came with this unique twist, my trajectory was a bit different than most children's. It seemed like every other week, I'd find myself in a cast, on crutches, or using my wheelchair, the result of another tumble or misadventure. My friends would play outside, climb trees, and engage in daring activities. For me, a simple misstep could lead to a fracture.

Now, most kids would be crushed by the constant physical setbacks, but it was something more for me. Each time I broke a bone, my world temporarily crumbled. I'd wonder, "Why me? Why does this keep happening?" It was as if the universe had a vendetta against my happiness.

My pessimistic mindset was forged in those moments of pain and frustration. I began to expect the worst, not just from my bone-breaking escapades but from life itself. I'd think, "If something as simple as walking down the stairs can lead to a broken leg, what other disasters are lurking around the corner?"

As I grew older, this mentality stuck with me. It became a part of my identity. I saw myself as someone who was cursed to face constant adversity. The fear of the next calamity became a self-fulfilling prophecy, affecting my physical well-being and mental and emotional state.

However, years later, after suffering the consequences of this mindset, I rose like a phoenix from its ashes. I not only underwent a physical transformation, but my mind shifted to a new perspective and clarity. I realized that I could not continue to let past accidents define me.

I realized that I couldn't control the accidents, but I could control how I responded to them. That was my turning point. I embraced positivity and saw these experiences as part of my unique path. I acknowledged that breaking bones was unfortunate but also a testament to my resilient spirit. Instead of dwelling on the negative, I focused on the lessons each injury taught me about resilience and the human capacity to heal.

I grew stronger, not just physically but mentally. The pain, frustration, and slow progress became stepping stones on my path to a more optimistic outlook.

I began to view life's challenges differently. Instead of seeing them as insurmountable obstacles, I saw them as opportunities for growth. Just as my bones mended and grew stronger after each break, so did my spirit.

The #UNBREAKABLE Power of Optimism

Uncovering the fantastic benefits of being an optimist will help you see that it's like a cascade of positivity that changes your life from the inside out:

- **Lower Stress Levels:** When you choose optimism, you don't let stress take the wheel. You navigate challenges with grace and resilience, knowing you can conquer anything life throws your way.

- **Improved Coping Skills:** Optimists face adversity head-on. Instead of crumbling under pressure, they rise to the occasion and find creative solutions to their problems.

- **Higher Energy Levels:** Positivity charges your batteries. When you're an optimist, you exude an infectious energy that keeps you going strong.

- **Increased Resilience:** For optimists, bouncing back from setbacks becomes second nature. They don't let a single stumble define them.

- **Enhanced Creativity:** Optimism sparks creativity. Your mind opens to new ideas and possibilities, paving the way for innovation.

- **Improved Wellbeing:** With a positive outlook, you foster a deep sense of well-being within yourself. Your mind and body find harmony, and you feel truly alive.

- **Reduced Pain and Depression**: Positivity eases your emotional burden, reducing feelings of pain and depression. It's like a healing balm for your soul.

How to Unlock Your Inner Optimist

Fired up and ready to harness the mighty force of optimism? Let me show you exactly what to do to consistently tap into your inner optimist:

#1 – Start Your Day with Positivity: Kickstart your day with a mantra, a motivating quote, or an uplifting song. It sets the tone for your entire day.

Over the years, I developed a morning routine centered on positivity. It evolves as my circumstances change, but this is how it started. Every day, in the shower, I recited empowering affirmations. Phrases like "I am strong," "I am capable," and "I attract positivity" became my daily mantras. They acted as a shield against negativity, empowering me to face the challenges ahead with confidence and optimism.

#2 – Focus on One Area at a Time: Don't overwhelm yourself by trying to be optimistic about everything at once. Pick one area of your life, such as work, family, or self-improvement, and infuse it with positivity.

The shift was profound when I consciously decided to focus on one area of my life at a time. I chose to focus on my health and fitness first. Instead of dreading workouts, I began to see exercise as an opportunity to nourish my body and mind. Soon, I looked forward to my daily workout routine, and my energy levels soared. By applying optimism to one aspect of my life, the positive energy spilled over into other areas, like ripples in a pond.

#3 – Regularly Exercise: Exercise is your #UNBREAKABLE tonic. It floods your body with dopamine, the happy hormone, and boosts your energy and optimism.

As someone with a physical disability, I had to find ways to adapt my workouts to my abilities. Initially, it was challenging, and I doubted whether I could maintain a regular exercise routine. But as you know, I chose to disable my disability and not let it define me; instead, I focused on what I could do.

Exercise became my anchor of positivity, a reminder that my body could do remarkable things. It empowered me to embrace my disability and find strength in every aspect of my life.

You Hold the Power

Here's the cold, hard truth: staying positive is an #UNBREAKABLE choice. We can't control all the negativity in the world, but we can control our response. Embrace the power of optimism, and you'll witness some major positive changes start to happen in your life.

When life throws you a curveball, remember that you get to choose how it affects you. As an optimist, you'll find the silver lining and seek solutions to any challenge.

It's time to push aside pessimism and let optimism take the wheel. You've got the superpower within you, and it's time to show it to the world. Embrace the positivity and watch how quickly you become #UNBREAKABLE!

Chapter 36

Baby Steps Versus Massive Action

As I've ventured into personal development, I've encountered many strategies and philosophies from the greats (and some not-so-greats) on maximizing productivity. I've faced both failures and moments of triumph. Among the many ideas I've explored, two have stood out like shining stars: Baby Steps versus Massive Action. These are on opposite sides of the spectrum and spark fiery discussions. It's like a clash of the Titans, with two powerful approaches to getting things done. The good news is, I'm here to tell you that both can lead to success, but let's explore the dynamics of each and how they fit into living an #UNBREAKABLE life.

The Baby Steps Treadmill: Slow and Cautious

Once upon a time, I was the poster child for taking baby steps. There I was, tiptoeing cautiously toward my goals, analyzing every move and ensuring everything was perfect before taking the next step. Baby steps are about caution, thinking things through, and feeling like you're doing something extraordinary. The only catch? It can take forever to achieve anything substantial.

I remember when I decided to prioritize my health, which was incredibly challenging because of my disability. I spent months planning, strategizing, and getting every detail just right. My careful approach made me feel like I was progressing, but I was stuck on a treadmill (pun intended) of inaction.

The Baby Steps approach sneakily makes us feel sensible, but more often than not, it holds us back. We get so caught up in perfecting everything that we lose sight of the bigger picture.

The Illusion of Perfection: Breaking Free

Baby steps might give us the illusion of perfection, but here's the truth I've discovered along the way: none of us are perfect, and perfection is a mirage. Embracing our imperfections is a crucial step in being #UNBREAKABLE.

Now, I was born with a disability, and for the longest time, I let the idea of being perfect hold me hostage. I thought, "If I can't do this perfectly, why bother?" It wasn't until I embraced my imperfections, turning them into strengths, that I truly understood the power of being #UNBREAKABLE.

The real #UNBREAKABLE truth is that waiting for perfection keeps you stuck in one place forever. Life is about growth, and growth thrives in the uncertainty of taking risks and facing challenges head-on.

Massive Action: Bold Leaps to Success

Now, let's switch gears to the world of massive action. Imagine yourself charging full speed ahead toward your goals like a fearless warrior, with no hesitations, no second-guessing, just going all-in. Massive action is about saying "yes" to opportunities, seizing the moment, and taking those daring leaps of faith.

I first came across the idea of massive action from the great Tony Robbins, and it hit me like a lightning bolt. The notion of going big without waiting for the stars to align resonated deeply with me. Massive action is about getting into action quickly, even if things aren't perfect.

Thinking back to when I wrote my book, "Disable Your Disability," I had been pondering the idea for about four years prior. I was stuck in wanting it to be perfect. I would jot down notes and ideas about the stories I wanted to share and the ideas I wanted to convey, and I did this for so long that I finally felt the pressure of my stalling. I tried using the baby steps method, and it wasn't working.

When I finally chose to sit down and write the book, I opted for massive action. Instead of meticulously planning every chapter, I dove headfirst into writing with passion and purpose. Of course, it wasn't perfect from the start, and I missed a few details here and there. But you know what? I was moving forward, making progress, and learning along the way.

Embrace Imperfect Action: Progress Over Perfection

The beauty of massive action is that it propels you forward. You're making genuine progress toward your goals, even if you miss a detail or two. It's like igniting a rocket's engines—you're soaring toward the stars.

I've seen this in my own life over and over again. When I decided to pursue my dream of becoming a motivational speaker, I didn't wait for everything to be perfect. I took massive action, started making and releasing videos online, booked speaking engagements, and shared my message with the world. I stumbled along the way, but each stumble taught me invaluable lessons that I wouldn't have learned if I had stayed stuck in the planning phase.

It's crucial to recognize that progress is more valuable than perfection. With massive action, you learn and grow through experience, gaining wisdom as you go. Every challenge becomes an opportunity to refine your approach and get closer to your dreams.

Finding Your Balance: Blending Baby Steps and Massive Action

You might wonder, "Should I go for baby steps or massive action?" It's not an either-or situation. You can find a balance that works for you.

In my life, I've learned to blend both approaches. I use baby steps when I need to plan and strategize, ensuring a solid foundation for my goals. Then, when the time is right, I move into massive action to charge forward fearlessly.

At the core of both baby steps and massive action lies the same magic ingredient—ACTION. A clear target goal plus taking action is the #UNBREAKABLE formula for success. Whether a little step or a giant leap, the key is to keep moving forward, no matter what.

So ask yourself—what steps can you take right now to move toward your dreams? What are you waiting for? Don't let fear or the illusion of perfection hold you back. Embrace your imperfections, take a deep breath, and charge forward with unyielding determination.

Remember, it's not about getting it right the first time—it's about daring to take that leap of faith. Be the hero of your story, embrace action, and unlock the door to #UNBREAKABLE success.

How I Did It

Let me share a personal story that embodies the power of combining baby steps and massive action to being #UNBREAKABLE.

When I first decided to prioritize my health, I faced a dilemma because of my fragile bones. Exercising and pushing myself seemed daunting, given my condition. I started cautiously. So much so that I didn't start exercising right away. I started researching. I was asking questions, trying to find answers. "How much exercise can I do with Osteogenesis Imperfecta?" "How can I avoid breaking my bones while exercising?" "What are exercises I can do if I have fragile bones?"

There were some very basic and general answers on the internet. There was little to no documentation or conversations about this topic as it pertained to Osteogenesis Imperfecta. It was primarily geared toward Osteoporosis; although they are both "fragile bones" conditions, they are very different otherwise. Even within my own O.I. Community, this topic appeared taboo, and most of my fellow O.I.ers were avoiding it.

So, I had to figure it out for myself. I had to take action.

I started moving more and doing low-impact activities that wouldn't strain my bones. I realized it was laying a solid foundation for me. These baby steps made me feel like I was progressing safely, but I soon realized they weren't enough.

I had to pivot toward massive action to see real progress, especially in my nutrition and mindset. It was a moment of clarity, like a lightning bolt of inspiration. Massive action meant wholeheartedly embracing a change in my diet, exercise routine, and mental attitude.

I remember the day I decided to shift my nutrition profoundly. Instead of tiptoeing around the idea, I dove in, revamping my diet to prioritize foods that fortified my bones and overall health. It wasn't a perfect start, and I stumbled in the process, but I was actively making strides toward my goal.

The same applied to my mindset. I couldn't afford to be hesitant or cautious in changing my attitude toward my disability. I had to dive in headfirst, reshaping my perspective and learning to leverage my condition as a source of strength and resilience.

The combination and beautiful marriage of baby steps and massive action propelled my health journey. The cautious beginning provided a sturdy foundation, while the bold leaps introduced me to new horizons of well-being. I wasn't trapped in the cycle of stagnation, nor was I recklessly charging forward without a plan. Instead, I had struck a harmonious balance between the two approaches.

The result? An #UNBREAKABLE transformation. My health improved, my mindset evolved, and I stood as living proof that combining baby steps with massive action can lead to extraordinary outcomes. I learned that perfection is a mirage and progress is the true measure of success.

Whether you choose baby steps or massive action, remember that what truly matters is that you're advancing toward your dreams.

You Have the Power

You hold the key to your #UNBREAKABLE destiny, so it doesn't matter which path of action you choose; but you have to choose one of them. You have to get into action. And when you do, the universe will conspire to guide you.

In my own #UNBREAKABLE journey, I've learned that it's not about getting it perfect—it's about getting it done. So, release your fears, break free from the chains of perfection, and get after your greatness.

You are an #UNBREAKABLE force, and the world awaits your brilliance. So, step out into the unknown, embrace the thrill of action, and live your #UNBREAKABLE life to the fullest!

Chapter 37

The Power of Support

One topic crucial to achieving an #UNBREAKABLE life is asking for help. I understand it can be challenging to check your pride at the door, but embracing help can be a huge step that propels you toward your dreams and goals.

The Pride Predicament: Breaking Free

Asking for help can be challenging. We've all been there. We often think we can do it all on our own. We want to prove ourselves to others and show the world we're self-reliant, resilient, and capable. But here's the thing—there's no shame in asking for help.

In my own #UNBREAKABLE story, I learned this valuable lesson at a critical point. When I chose to transform my physical health and embrace a healthier lifestyle, I thought I could do it alone. Due to my disability, I had spent years fending for myself, and I wanted to prove to myself and others that I could handle it all.

But guess what? That was a recipe for frustration and stagnation. I call it "the gap" - the period between deciding to change and taking action. I was stuck in this gap, trying to figure it all out on my own, searching online, and watching numerous YouTube videos for solutions, but still not progressing.

Asking for help requires vulnerability, and it's not always easy to admit that we can't do it alone. We might fear being perceived as weak, incapable, or inexperienced. But let me assure you, asking for help takes immense courage. It shows that you're willing to take ownership of your story and understand the value of collaboration and support.

Realization and Liberation: Embracing Support

The turning point came when I finally admitted that I needed help. It wasn't a sign of weakness but a sign of strength—the strength to recognize my limitations and seek assistance to overcome them.

It was my moment of clarity. I acknowledged that I couldn't achieve my vision alone. I had to set aside my pride, embrace vulnerability, and open myself up to seeking help from others.

I want you to understand that asking for help doesn't mean you're incapable or inexperienced. It's about acknowledging that achieving greatness requires a team effort. None of us can do it all alone, and that's perfectly okay.

Navigating Rejection and Low Expectations

As much as collaboration is powerful, it's essential to recognize that not everyone can or is willing to offer help when needed. There will be times when you reach out, and others may not come through for various reasons. This is where managing expectations becomes crucial.

We cannot let the fear of being let down hold us back from asking for help. On one hand, if we worry too much about someone not providing help, we may never ask for it. On the other hand, if we expect too much from someone and they don't come through, we'll end up discouraged and upset. Either way, when we learn to manage our expectations and understand that we cannot control the actions of others, we clear the way for us to have the courage to ask for help regardless of the outcome. And that's how you infuse #UNBREAKABLE power in asking for help!

A Powerful Step

My life took a monumental leap forward when I finally asked for help and sought guidance from professionals, mentors, and like-minded individuals. It confirmed that asking for help doesn't make you weak—it makes you wise. It opens doors to new perspectives, insights, and possibilities you may not have considered alone.

I hired a personal trainer and sought the assistance of my wife, who had been on her healthy living journey for a few years and had been doing her best to encourage me along the way. I also started hanging around other people who made their health a priority.

The conversations changed. My focus changed. My daily habits changed. Everything moved in the right direction quickly. I not only found myself feeling stronger physically, but I felt that my decision-making powers became stronger. By leaning into what my coaches and mentors were advising, I started to see that expanding my perspectives would allow me to reach my greatness faster.

Building an #UNBREAKABLE Support Network

Asking for help isn't just about one-time assistance; it's about creating a support network that sustains and uplifts you throughout your journey. I've discovered this in every professional endeavor I've pursued. From video production to motivational speaking, from DJing to writing and publishing books, collaboration and connecting with like-minded people have been crucial in my success.

Many of these individuals have become my mentors, cheerleaders, and sounding boards. We celebrated each other's successes, shared resources, and encouraged each other during challenging times. It's been a beautiful give-and-take that strengthened our collective pursuit of greatness.

Unleashing the Power of Collaboration

I encourage you to take a moment and reflect. Where do you feel stuck in your life, right on the verge of a breakthrough, but something's holding you back? That's the moment to consider asking for help. Seek out the right mentors and allies who can guide and support you. Embrace the vulnerability that comes with asking for help, knowing it is a source of strength.

Greatness is not a solo project. It's a collective effort in which we lift each other up and propel one another toward success. So don't be afraid to seek guidance, share your dreams with others, and create a support network. It's not about pride or ego; it's about recognizing that we're all in this together.

Remember, you can be self-reliant, resilient, and strong while still seeking support from others. Collaboration is magic, and together, we can achieve more than we ever thought possible.

Chapter 38

Getting Unstuck

Breaking free from feeling stuck is an important skill to learn as you become #UNBREAKABLE. We've all experienced those moments when life seems to grind to a halt, trapping us in an endless loop of frustration. It could be as minor as getting stuck in a traffic jam or as significant as feeling trapped in a job or relationship that drains your happiness. The good news is that we all possess the power to peel ourselves free from these sticky situations.

Understanding the Different Levels of Feeling Stuck

Feeling stuck comes in various forms, and each level demands a different approach to breaking free. Let's look at these levels to help gain some clarity.

Level 1 stuck is like getting caught in a traffic jam. It's inconvenient and frustrating, but it's usually easy to escape. You wait for the traffic to clear, and soon, you're on your way again. Or perhaps you get home and realize you received the wrong meal in your drive-thru bag. It's annoying, sure, but relatively easy to wriggle out of. Similarly, life's minor hiccups can sometimes temporarily slow us down, but they don't hold us captive.

Level 2 stuck is more complex. It's when you find yourself in situations or relationships that drain your energy and enthusiasm. Breaking free from this level of being stuck requires more effort and determination. It's like being in a job you dislike, knowing you're capable of so much more but feeling trapped.

Then, there's Level 3—the most challenging and dangerous form of being stuck. At this level, you might not even realize that you're trapped. It's like drifting through life, year after year, without realizing you're caught in a never-ending cycle of comfort and routine. You become so used to feeling uncomfortable that you no longer question it. Others might even attempt to convince you that you're stuck, but your reality has been reshaped, and you don't see a way out. Or worse yet, you can't accept that you're stuck.

We may or may not be responsible for getting stuck, but we are responsible for getting ourselves out when we realize that a change needs to happen.

Telltale signs of being stuck are being unhappy, depressed, unmotivated, and more than likely feeling that we're not living up to our full potential.

Uncovering My Stuck Moments

Now, you might think that someone like me, who has faced the challenges of living with a rare bone disorder, would have mastered the art of breaking free from feeling stuck. However, I've had my share of Level 3 stuck moments.

My journey from being a fragile child in a wheelchair to a guy who relied on crutches and finally to walking unaided was a significant achievement. However, I soon discovered a new kind of entrapment. I grew up listening to the words "be careful." Unfortunately, as I grew up and started living my adult life, these two simple words echoed endlessly in my mind, paralyzing me with fear. I was afraid to do anything physical. And because of that, my health suffered.

After breaking through my personal barriers and transforming my entire life, I looked back and identified the key steps that helped me reclaim it. Now, I'd like to share those with you.

No matter how stuck you may feel, there is a way out!

Step #1 - Honesty—The Path to Clarity

Breaking free from feeling stuck begins with one simple truth—acknowledging that you're stuck. It's time to be honest with yourself, to drop the masks and excuses, especially the ones we tell ourselves. There may be parts of your story that you can't change, just like my disability, but you can always choose how you respond to your circumstances. Embrace and be honest with your reality; you'll find the path to freedom.

Step #2 - Willingness—The Spark of Action

Wanting change is passive; being willing to change is the first step to taking action. Set aside your fears and comfort zones, and you'll tap into an incredible energy source within you. Being willing is the catalyst that propels you from "maybe someday" to "right now." It's the moment you decide you're no longer content with being stuck and are ready to move forward.

Step #3 - Seek Help—Navigating the Unknown

As you begin breaking free from feeling stuck, you'll venture into uncharted territory. Seeking guidance is not a sign of weakness but a mark of strength. Just as I enlisted a personal trainer to guide my physical transformation, find mentors, therapists, or advisors who can help you navigate the complexities of change. Their expertise can fast-track your path to liberation.

Step #4 – Embrace Faith—Trust the Process

Have faith in yourself and the process. Believe in what you can't see yet. Remember, the most remarkable journeys often begin with a single step, and you may not always see the entire path ahead. As you begin, with each small step, you'll prove to yourself that you can change. Acknowledge these accomplishments, and you will instill faith in yourself. With faith in your potential and the power of change, you'll have the courage to challenge your limitations.

Writing Your Unstuck Narrative

The next time you feel stuck, don't surrender. Instead, declare, "I'm stuck right now. How do I get myself out of this?" Whether you're stuck at Level 1, 2, or 3, the path to freedom begins with your decision to take that first step. Your life is yours to reclaim, and an #UNBREAKABLE future awaits you on the other side of feeling stuck.

Chapter 39

The #UNBREAKABLE Trinity

Let's explore a foundational thought regarding improving our lives: the #UNBREAKABLE Trinity: Motivation, Inspiration, and Discipline. These three powerful forces are essential for crafting an #UNBREAKABLE life, and I'm here to clarify each one's significance for you. So, let's get right into it!

Motivation – Fueled by Desire

Motivation is the driving force that sparks your willingness to take action. It's that fire within you, fueled by desire, pushing you to achieve your goals. Think of motivation as your inner cheerleader, urging you to stay focused and keep moving forward. It's like a constant companion, whispering words of encouragement during challenging times and celebrating your victories with unbridled enthusiasm. With motivation by your side, you'll find the strength to conquer self-doubt and overcome any adversity that comes your way.

Motivation has been a game-changer in my life, especially as I started getting and staying healthy with my disability. Every time I start a workout, I desire to better myself and provide myself with what I need to feel more energetic and strong. Motivation gets me out of bed each morning, ready to face the day enthusiastically; whether I have a list of tasks to complete or a quiet day for myself.

Inspiration - Stimulated by Feelings

On the other hand, Inspiration is the process of being emotionally stimulated to do or feel something. It's the emotional force that propels you into action, often sparked by witnessing something extraordinary or touching. Inspiration breathes life into your dreams and fuels your creativity like a gentle breeze that carries your aspirations higher and higher. When you find yourself immersed in inspiration, the possibilities seem endless, and you become receptive to new ideas and perspectives. It's that "aha" moment when clarity dawns, and you feel a surge of purpose, ready to embrace the world with your unique vision.

As a motivational speaker, I'm often called an inspiration, and I embrace that title with gratitude. Knowing that my story as someone with a disability inspires others to push past their limits fills my heart with joy. I've learned that while motivation can ignite a spark, inspiration keeps that flame burning long after the moment has passed.

Discipline – The Power of Consistency

Discipline is the glue that holds the trinity together. It's all about training yourself to obey the rules you set for yourself and creating a routine that fosters growth and success. Discipline ensures you stay committed to your goals, even when motivation and inspiration seem elusive. It acts as a guiding force, steering you back on track when distractions or challenges try to veer you off course. With discipline, you build the resilience to push through obstacles, knowing that every step you take brings you closer to your #UNBREAKABLE self.

I've witnessed the incredible impact of discipline in my brother Rob's life. He's older than me by three years and has diligently worked out and stayed active for years. His unwavering discipline in maintaining a healthy lifestyle has kept him fit and healthy.

My wife, Teemaree, is doing the same, and I see the results she gets because she seems to be going backward in time with each passing year! Discipline keeps my brother and wife going, even when life gets busy or obstacles arise. They both inspire me to maintain discipline in my fitness and healthy living.

The Power of the #UNBREAKABLE Trinity

Here's the magic: these three elements form an #UNBREAKABLE trinity. They are interconnected and work harmoniously to propel you toward your goals. While each has its unique role, they complement and reinforce one another. Let's break it down:

- **Motivation** is the initial spark, igniting your desire to take action.

- **Inspiration** fans the spark into a burning flame, creating emotional connections to your dreams.

- **Discipline** is the backbone, providing consistency and structure to keep you on track.

Here's a fun way to remember this principle: Imagine this trinity as a dance, with motivation being the music leading the way, inspiration being your love for the movement, and discipline bringing it all together in beautiful, coordinated steps. When you feel unmotivated, inspiration swoops in to remind you of your passion, and discipline keeps you moving forward.

I used this powerful trinity to build both my Disable Your Disability and #UNBREAKABLE movements. My motivation to inspire others with disabilities and inspiration from those I encountered led to unwavering discipline in my mission. Together, they form an

#UNBREAKABLE bond that propels me forward despite setbacks and challenges.

Your Unique Formula for #UNBREAKABLE Success

In my life, I found that while motivation helps me start projects, inspiration keeps me going, and discipline ensures I see them through to completion. Embrace your journey, and remember that it's okay to adjust the balance of the trinity as needed.

There's no one-size-fits-all formula for harnessing the power of the #UNBREAKABLE trinity. You get to create your unique ratio of motivation, inspiration, and discipline, like a chemist blending the perfect concoction of determination and drive. Experiment and discover what works best for you. Find your personalized blend. Embrace the ebb and flow of life, knowing that motivation may sometimes take center stage while inspiration leads the way for others. Allow discipline to be the constant foundation that steadies your course, like a compass pointing true north. As you work with it, you'll find the sweet spot where productivity meets fulfillment and your dreams become reality.

Chapter 40

Does It Have to Be Hard?

Life-changing projects, especially self-discovery, often come to a screeching halt at the mere thought of difficulty. We hit roadblocks when the prospect of something being hard looms large in our minds. Whether it's the daunting nature of an entire endeavor or the challenging moments throughout, the perception of difficulty can paralyze our progress.

Consider the notion of time—a precious commodity that governs our decisions. The fear of wasting time often becomes a significant deterrent. Learning something new, which might require a substantial investment of time, triggers frustration. We feel we're missing out on other aspects of life, and in response, we abandon our pursuits.

It's crucial to recognize that the concept of difficulty is highly subjective. Much like the ambiguity of "expensive" or "cheap" when assessing a purchase, labeling something as hard or easy lacks objectivity. What proves challenging for one person might be a breeze for another. It's a matter of individual perspective.

Just as asking, "How much did it cost?" might yield subjective responses, asking, "Was it hard or difficult?" can lead to similarly subjective answers. The key to overcoming challenges is shifting our mindset around what is considered hard.

Do things inherently have to be hard? To live an #UNBREAKABLE life, the answer is a resounding "no!" Our perception of difficulty is often a self-imposed barrier, particularly in learning. We've conditioned ourselves to believe that acquiring new skills or knowledge is arduous. However, the truth is that only the things we don't wish to do become burdensome. If you truly want to do something, you'll learn it and do it without considering how difficult it is to accomplish.

So, how can we redefine our perspective on challenges?

#1 – Assume Ease

Before diving into any task, cultivate a mindset that anticipates ease. Convince yourself that it's going to be straightforward. The power of positive expectation can significantly impact your experience. Assuming ease is like providing yourself with a mental roadmap for success. When you cultivate a mindset that anticipates ease, you're setting your mind up to embrace challenges as opportunities rather than insurmountable hurdles.

This positive expectation acts as a catalyst, influencing your approach to tasks with a sense of confidence and preparedness. Imagine it as a mental warm-up before a physical workout — by assuming ease; you're ensuring that your mental faculties are flexible, resilient, and ready to adapt to the twists and turn that any endeavor might present. This proactive mental stance fosters a smoother path and positions you to navigate complexities with a clarity that changes challenges into stepping stones toward personal and professional growth.

#2 – Break It Down

When facing a monumental change, like an entire life overhaul, avoid letting the grandeur of the goal overwhelm you. Break it down into smaller, manageable goals. Achieving these milestones boosts your confidence and mitigates the perceived difficulty associated with time. Breaking down monumental changes into smaller, manageable goals adds another level to your structured roadmap for success. This strategic approach lets you deconstruct what might seem impossible tasks into bite-sized, achievable milestones.

These smaller goals act as progress markers, guiding you through the change and providing a tangible sense of accomplishment at each step. Moreover, by focusing on manageable portions, you effectively bypass the overwhelm often accompanying significant life changes. This process boosts confidence and reshapes your perception of time, making the overall endeavor feel more approachable and less daunting. It's a powerful technique that shifts the seemingly impossible into a series of achievable steps, fostering a sense of empowerment and resilience.

#3 – Visualize Success

Whenever the going gets tough, get tough and get going by actively engaging in visualization. Imagine yourself on the other side of the challenge, enjoying the fruits of the accomplishment. Fully embrace the positive emotions associated with the change you're working toward. Visualization acts as a potent mental rehearsal, allowing you to pre-experience success before it even happens. When facing challenges, close your eyes and imagine the scenario where you've triumphed over the difficulty. Picture the joy, satisfaction, and accomplishment in detail.

This mental imagery is a source of motivation and mental conditioning, preparing your mind for success. It helps you stay focused on your goals and instills a positive emotional connection to the change you're striving for. Visualization is a proactive tool that turns your aspirations into a vivid reality within your mind, nurturing the belief that success is not just achievable but inevitable.

By altering our perception of what's hard, we can navigate challenges with greater ease. Redefining difficulty as a subjective experience and adopting a positive mindset can lead to new experiences beyond our wildest dreams.

Remember, the task is not inherently hard; our mindset determines the difficulty level. So, change how you define what's hard, and witness how effortlessly you can become #UNBREAKABLE in the face of any challenge.

An #UNBREAKABLE Invitation

Congratulations! What a ride!! Forty powerful pieces of solid advice.

You've come a long way, and now, it's time to embrace your #UNBREAKABLE power!

But remember, this is just the beginning—there's so much more in store for you!

We are all a work in progress, continually learning, growing, and improving every day.

Now, let me extend a heartfelt invitation that could be the turning point in your life—a call to the next phase to propel you even further. Are you ready to seize the opportunity and rise to new heights? Are you eager to apply all that you've learned to real-life situations and experience profound and positive changes?

Then it's time for action!

And it all happens at my website;
www.tonyjacobsen.com
and/or www.advicetobeunbreakable.com

Imagine having your own personal guide—a coach who understands your unique challenges, dreams, and aspirations. I can offer you that beyond this book.

With one-on-one coaching, we'll explore your path's intricacies, uncover your capabilities, and maximize your strengths. Together, we'll craft a personalized roadmap to your version of greatness, ensuring that every step you take aligns with your grand vision.

Perhaps you crave the energy of a supportive community—the kindred spirits who cheer you on, celebrate your wins, and lend a helping hand when you need it most. In that case, group coaching is the answer. Surround yourself with like-minded individuals who are striving to break free from limitations and live an #UNBREAKABLE life. The power of collective growth is nothing short of magical, and you'll find yourself inspired and motivated in ways you never thought possible.

And for those of you who love the flexibility of learning at your own pace, there are online courses that are tailor-made for you. These courses are not just ordinary lessons—they are life-altering experiences designed to empower you with the tools and knowledge you need to conquer any challenge that comes your way. Dive into the wealth of expertise, actionable insights, and transformative exercises, and witness your life taking a new, exhilarating trajectory.

When you visit the website, you'll find a treasure trove of resources—a safe space where you can find guidance, inspiration, and motivation anytime. From insightful blog posts to motivational videos, from downloadable workbooks to interactive workshops, there's something for every #UNBREAKABLE warrior seeking growth and self-mastery.

Now, you might be thinking, "Do I need assistance? Can't I do this on my own?" The truth is, the trek to an #UNBREAKABLE life is an expedition best shared. Just like the world's greatest athletes rely on coaches to enhance their performance, having a guiding hand will significantly elevate your experience. It's the difference between good and exceptional, between progress and monumental breakthroughs.

Remember, asking for help isn't a sign of weakness—it's a testament to your strength and commitment to growth. When you seek support, you open yourself to unlimited possibilities, and the world responds positively.

So, don't hesitate any longer. Don't waste another day, hour, or minute of your life. Embrace the special invitation, and let's continue this adventure together.

Say yes to investing in yourself and your future, and watch as the world conspires to bring forth your greatness. With the proper support and resources, there's no limit to what you can achieve. Let's shatter any remaining barriers you may have and soar to new heights.

Scan the QR code at the end of this chapter right now to explore the wealth of opportunities that await you. Whether you're interested in one-on-one coaching, group coaching, transformative online courses, or live workshops, take that leap of faith and take control of your destiny.

About the Author

Tony Jacobsen, a seasoned author/writer, renowned speaker, and certified personal trainer, began his writing journey fueled by a passion for empowering individuals to overcome obstacles and lead fulfilling lives. Inspired by his personal transformative experience, Tony penned his debut book, "Disable Your Disability: Live the Healthy Life You Deserve!" His latest offering, "Advice to be #UNBREAKABLE," is a beacon of hope, guiding readers toward embracing their uniqueness and cultivating resilience through practical steps.

With a wealth of accolades in public speaking and health coaching, including multiple prestigious awards, Tony has impacted countless lives. He coaches and guides individuals to achieve and maintain optimal health despite their limitations. His dynamic speaking style and compassionate approach resonate deeply with audiences worldwide.

Beyond his literary and speaking endeavors, Tony finds creative expression through DJing and music production, creating mixes and melodies that uplift, motivate, and make you move. A massive fan of "Star Wars" and "Indiana Jones," he loves film and writes spec screenplays when the muse appears. His favorite television show, "The Office," is a source of endless laughter and relatability. He's watched the series 20+ times through! Tony is also a total animal lover: cats, dogs, goats—in that order.

Tony thrives on exploring the intersection of innovation and wellness. When not immersed in his work, he treasures moments spent traveling with his beloved wife, immersing themselves in new cultures and experiences. With an insatiable curiosity and a genuine passion for helping others, Tony continues to leave an indelible mark on the world, one #UNBREAKABLE word at a time.